The Gospel according
to Bruce Springsteen

The Gospel according to Bruce Springsteen

Rock and Redemption, from *Asbury Park* to *Magic*

Jeffrey B. Symynkywicz

2008

Westminster John Knox Press

LOUISVILLE • LONDON

Scripture quotations from the New Revised Standard Version of the Bible are copyright © 1989 by the Division of Christian Education of the National Council of the Churches of Christ in the U.S.A. and are used by permission.

Book design by Sharon Adams
Cover design by designpointinc.com
Cover photograph: © *David Bergman/Corbis*

First edition
Published by Westminster John Knox Press
Louisville, Kentucky

This book is printed on acid-free paper that meets the American National Standards Institute Z39.48 standard. ♾

PRINTED IN THE UNITED STATES OF AMERICA

08 09 10 11 12 13 14 15 16 17 — 10 9 8 7 6 5 4 3 2 1

Library of Congress Cataloging-in-Publication Data

Symynkywicz, Jeffrey.
The Gospel according to Bruce Springsteen : rock and redemption, from Asbury Park to Magic / Jeffrey B. Symynkywicz. — 1st ed.
p. cm.
Includes bibliographical references (p.).
ISBN 978-0-664-23169-9 (alk. paper)
1. Springsteen, Bruce—Criticism and interpretation. 2. Rock music—United States—Religious aspects—Christianity. I. Title.

ML420.S77.S96 2008
782.42166092—dc22

2007046610

For Elizabeth,

again and forever.

"If I should fall behind,
Wait for me."

Contents

Introduction

The Ministry of Rock and Roll

*D*evotees of different religious systems often have truly amazing miracle stories to relate. Here's mine.

In the summer of 2004, my wife, Elizabeth, and I were nearing the end of our first full day as travelers in southeastern France. We were sitting in an ornately decorated dining room in a charming hotel on the main street in Corps, a small town about forty miles south of Grenoble, just on the edge of the French Alps. We had returned a short time before from a sometimes harrowing, always exhilarating, thoroughly rewarding excursion over about ten miles of arduous mountain roads to the shrine of Notre Dame de LaSalette, which sits perched on a mountainside about six thousand feet above Corps.

Now, having survived the drive down the mountain, it was time for dinner. At the shrine, we had heard good things from another American traveler about this restaurant in the village, at the Hotel de la Poste; we were not disappointed. For more than two hours, we luxuriated in the bounty of French cuisine: there had been *escargots*, and *champignons*, and *confit de canard;* rich chocolate desserts, and fine local cheeses. Now, sated and full, it was almost time for us to go, and as Elizabeth paid a visit to the powder room and I waited for our check over coffee, I happened to hear the music that was playing softly over the restaurant's speakers. It was Bruce Springsteen's "Streets of Philadelphia." I smiled, shook my head, and pondered how uncanny it was to be sitting here, in a small village, in this isolated corner of France, hearing my hero, Springsteen, coming over the speakers singing a song about Philadelphia, back in the

States. Not Springsteen's most romantic song, I thought; but still, the irony was quite amazing.

As Elizabeth rejoined me, I called her attention to the music. We smiled and shared a little laugh as Bruce finished up the song. After a brief pause the next song came on, and in a few moments we were both in tears.

That next song was "our" song (or, at least, the most recent incarnation of "our" song). It was Bruce again, this time singing "If I Should Fall Behind," a song we both love and had come to see as a symbol for us, of our marriage, our love for one another, and our common journey. "If I should fall behind," the singer asks his beloved, "wait for me." Wherever we travel in life—wherever life takes us—we will wait for one another and hold one another close.

It was a moment that could not have been scripted better. Here we were, traveling side by side on this trip of a lifetime—a trip we had talked about taking for so many years—celebrating the jubilee year of our common journey of twenty-five years. With us now was Bruce Springsteen, an unseen (but not unheard) traveling companion, singing about faith and fidelity and love and loyalty.

Bruce had been there for us before. On other critical milestones along our journey, he had provided vital notes in the "soundtrack of our lives," to use Dick Clark's insightful phrase.

I can remember the first time I ever heard Springsteen's music. It was in the spring of 1976 at Elizabeth's senior prom at the Chateau de Ville supper club in Framingham, Massachusetts. The band played "Thunder Road," which had just been released a year or so before as part of the *Born to Run* album. We danced and danced, and one line from that song—"Your graduation gown lies in rags at their feet"—seemed somehow so appropriate to the occasion that it carved a place into my memory.

We danced to other Springsteen numbers that night as well. I remember hearing the references to Crazy Janey and the Mission Man in his "Spirit in the Night," wondering if the parallels to the poems about Crazy Jane and the Bishop by William Butler Yeats were intentional. (I'm still wondering.) Soon Elizabeth and I were hooked on Springsteen, and in the spring of 1977, we celebrated her recovery from mononucleosis by going to see him at the Music Hall in Boston, back when he was still not quite a megastar and was still playing relatively small theaters and not huge sports arenas.

But the years intervened, and in time, we put aside some of the trappings of our younger, somewhat more carefree years. As family responsibilities and the raising of children came to the fore, our ardor for "the Boss" cooled somewhat, and the importance of his music receded into the background. The soundtrack faded to a soft background melody, though we did hold on to our old LPs and would take them out, dust them off, and play them from time to time.

But the notes of that original rendition of "Thunder Road" were merely lying in wait—waiting for a later, and even bolder, reprise.

It came as we were taking our oldest son, Micah, down to Baltimore to start his first year at Johns Hopkins University. Long car trips down the I-95 corridor of the American Northeast can be notoriously boring. By the time we reached the southern reaches of the New Jersey Turnpike, the miles seemed to be dragging along. The scenery consisted of toll booths and tarmac and taillights. There wasn't much of interest on the radio, and everyone else in the car seemed to have dozed off in the midday heat of late summer. Somewhere just before Delaware, I started rummaging through the cassette tapes we had brought along. I came across Springsteen's *Greatest Hits*, which I had bought a couple of years before but had played relatively few times since. The first song on the album was "Thunder Road."

Perhaps it was the pent-up emotion of taking my firstborn off to college. Or perhaps it was simply the monotony and exhaustion of a long car trip in the heat of summer. But all of a sudden, I found myself deeply affected by that relatively simple piece of music I had heard, no doubt, scores of times before. I felt goose bumps along my arm, tears welled up in my eyes, and my voice caught as I tried to sing along about a screen door slamming and Roy Orbison singing for the lonely.

Bruce was there, singing about graduation again—not graduation as a once-in-a-lifetime, here's-your-diploma, now-go-get-a-job event. Rather, he was singing about the many, continual graduations we face whenever we leave behind the well-worn (and perhaps constrictive and grown-too-small) ways of the past and dare to enter a new stage in our lives.

Bruce was there for us as we made our journey to the next stage of our life.

He would be there again, about a year later, on the morning after we buried my father, and I drove home alone, after dropping Micah off at the Providence airport for his flight back to Baltimore. As I listened to the words of the song "Independence Day" from the album *The River,* Bruce was once again summing up for me the inevitability of the transition I was now facing. "Well Papa, go to bed now, it's getting late," Bruce sang, and I thought of my own father, now eternally at rest. There comes for all of us that "Independence Day" when those who have nurtured us and loved us will be no more and with whom our relationship, for good or ill, is now history.

Once again, the tears fell. They were tears of loss, but tears of healing as well. And I sensed again that power deep within us to transcend the inevitable pain and heartache of the passing years and to carve out for ourselves meaningful, fulfilling, and loving lives.

Perhaps a large part of Springsteen's resilience—his enduring popularity over more than three decades now—is a sense among many of us that his music points toward something deeper and somehow essential to our lives. When we discern that Springsteen is "there" for us—when we feel as though he is addressing us directly and personally in his songs—his work seems to put down strong roots in our own experience. His music helps us to make sense of the sometimes tangled, often disparate threads of our lives. This is, at its foundation, a religious undertaking, a ministry of healing. The very word "religion," after all, is from the Latin *religare*, which means "to bind together again." It refers to that system, those perspectives, the overriding metaphorical and mythological scheme that binds things together for people—that provides them with a sense of meaning and transcendence. For many men and women, it is the work of Bruce Springsteen that either provides this canopy of meaning or that gives them fresh and vital tools for discerning it more clearly in their own chosen faith traditions.

But Springsteen's ministry is a distinctly *public* one as well. "Blessed is he who is joined to all the living," the book of Proverbs says. "All the living"—not just those we like, not just those like us, not just those favored by fortune or close to the centers of wealth, power, and prestige. Throughout his career, Springsteen has exhibited a brilliant ability to reflect the full scope and range of our human predicament. In an era when so much of our culture in general, and so much of contemporary music in particular, deals with trivialities, Springsteen continues to write about things that matter. "Springsteen has never wavered to sing the song of the disenfranchised and disregarded," Renee Graham of the *Boston Globe* has written.[1]

Even more, he has never flinched from pointing out to each of us those "disenfranchised and disregarded"—and fallen and broken and empty—aspects of our own souls as well.

"You and I know what this world can do," Springsteen reminded Elizabeth and me as we sat transfixed that summer evening at the little restaurant in southeastern France. We felt fully in love with one another and fully alive to the blessings of grace. But Springsteen's genius would never allow us to remain forever "blinded by the light" of each other's eyes. He would never let us forget that for those of us who have, there are those who do not; for all who rejoice, there are those who mourn; for all who hope, there are those who despair; for all of us whose lives have been fortunate and privileged, there are those for whom life has been too often oppressive and bleak.

But "like a catfish dancing on the end of my line" (to quote his song "The Rising"), he has never wavered in singing a defiantly hopeful song of life as well. Seldom in Springsteen's songs (as gritty and realistic and unsentimental as most of them are) is despair given the last word. With grace, courage, and resilience, the darkest night gives way to the morning, the deepest wounds find healing, and a glimmer of hope usually appears in even the most hopeless and dysfunctional situation.

Written clearly at the heart of the good news according to Bruce Springsteen is the affirmation that no principality or power—no forces seen or unseen, no terror-mad souls or devilish plots—can ever separate us from the love that is in our souls. As long as that love abides, so will hope, and through hope we can come to know the sustaining joy of human community on this good earth.

Almost every night during the momentous Reunion Tour of Springsteen with his E Street Band during 1999–2000, "the Boss" would speak exuberantly of "the power, the magic, the mystery, and the ministry of rock and roll." These lines were, for Bruce, neither mere showmanship nor empty bravado. They were for him, rather, gospel truth—a clear indication of how he pictured his relationship to his music and his fans. Close to the heart of Springsteen's art is the ability we all share to sense that power, contemplate that magic, and dance with that mystery.

In his epic series of conversations with the journalist Bill Moyers, the great scholar of mythology Joseph Campbell responded to one of Moyers's questions about "the meaning of life" by saying, "I don't think people are really seeking the meaning of Life. I think we're seeking an experience of being alive."[2] In a published and recorded body of work stretching back over thirty years now— over 250 songs in all, as listed on his official Web site[3]—Springsteen would seem to agree with Campbell. While he offers no final and definitive dictum on what it all means, he does proffer a remarkably vivid and varied portrayal on how wondrous and multifaceted our experience of aliveness can be.

In this present work, we will plumb the depths of this extensive canon. We will look in some detail at the "divine things, well enveloped" (in Whitman's phrase) in many (though by no means all, or even most) of those songs—songs that, of course, were meant to be *heard* more than read; songs in which, in most cases, the *music* is at least as important to the entire experience as the lyrics are. Perhaps this book, then, should be read with a CD player and the particular album(s) under consideration close at hand. Readers might also want to avail themselves of the full version of the lyrics to Springsteen's songs. The words of all of them are available on the official Web site, and those of earlier albums (through *The Ghost of Tom Joad*) are beautifully presented along with Bruce's comments in the oversized volume *Songs*.[4] The fair use doctrine allows the publication of only a smattering of lyrics from various songs here; to experience fully the vigor and nuance of Springsteen's writing style, one needs access to the complete lyrics of his songs.

"I can't promise you life everlasting," Springsteen would also say as part of his monologue during the Reunion Tour, "but I can promise you life *right now*."[5] "All—is the price of All," wrote Emily Dickinson. Only by grasping it *all*—in every aspect of its pain and beauty—can we truly know life. Only by heeding it all—in the lives and voices of all those around us—can we ever hear the Spirit calling to us.

In opening our eyes to the movement of life all around us, the words of Bruce Springsteen can allow us to glimpse, just a little more plainly, the ministrations of the Spirit across the face of our world. His words and music can allow us to discern the voice of the Spirit speaking in our souls just a little more clearly.

Chapter One

Welcome to the Fall
Greetings from Asbury Park, N.J.

Something is rotten in the state of New Jersey (as well as in parts of neighboring New York). Right from the start—from the hyperactive verbosity of the recording's first track, "Blinded by the Light"—Bruce Springsteen's first album, *Greetings from Asbury Park, N.J.* (1973) explodes with its troubled vision of a world gone awry. The decrepit reality of Asbury Park itself—a poor and deeply troubled city on the North Jersey shore, now far removed from its glory days depicted in the vintage tourist's postcard on the album's cover—serves as Springsteen's accessible and highly autobiographical metaphor for a world that is either falling or fallen. In *Greetings*, for the first time, we are introduced to Springsteen's vision of the world as a gritty, conflicted, oftentimes dark and sinister place—not unlike what Asbury Park itself has become. This unblinking, unsentimentalized picture of the world has evolved with time, of course; over the course of Springsteen's career, it has presented itself in a vast universe of different ways. But the grit and the conflict—and the darkness—has always been there. Always present, too, has been the kinetic charge of lives genuinely lived, as well as the liberating audacity of souls who refuse to surrender in the face of the travails they face.

Bruce Springsteen was born of working class parents in Long Branch, New Jersey, on September 23, 1949. He grew up in the blue-collar town of Freehold, about fifteen miles from the Jersey Shore, where his father was a truck driver and his mother a secretary. As a

1

boy, he attended the St. Rose of Lima parochial school but in ninth grade transferred to the public Freehold High School, where he had a markedly unexceptional career and from which he graduated in 1967.

That fall, Springsteen enrolled at Ocean Community College in Toms River, just down the road from Freehold. But college life wasn't for him, and he dropped out sometime during the first semester. Rather early on in life, he seems to have decided he would make his way as a musician. He had joined his first band, the Rogues, in 1964, at the age of fifteen. The next year, he joined the Castiles—a band that earned the princely sum of thirty-five dollars (split five ways) for playing at the local swim club in Woodhaven, New Jersey.[1] Now, a little more than a year out of high school, Springsteen and his new band, Steel Mill, traveled across the country to try to break into the music scene around San Francisco and Berkeley. But rather soon, Springsteen decided that he had no desire to remain in California; instead, he and the other members of Steel Mill returned to Asbury Park, where they continued to make a name for themselves playing in some of the numerous bars and clubs in towns along the Jersey Shore.

The world to which Springsteen was returning was far from prosperous: Asbury Park's once-booming vacation trade was in decline; by 1970, nearly thirty percent of the city's population was on welfare.[2] Relations between blacks and whites there, which had never been good, reached their nadir on the night of July 5, 1970, when fights broke out between rival gangs of black and white youths. These fights soon escalated into a full-scale race riot, which continued for the next four nights. Asbury Park never recovered.

It was in the midst of this descent of his adopted hometown into economic decline and racial turmoil—with the shattered dreams and decaying carnival amusements of Asbury Park as his evocative backdrop—that Bruce Springsteen composed the songs for his first album, most of them while he sat alone in an abandoned beauty parlor on the first floor beneath his apartment.[3]

Songs of a Not-so-Innocent Innocence

In the spring of 1972, John Hammond, a leading New York talent scout—a man who had previously helped to launch the careers of great musical figures such as Benny Goodman, Count Basie, Billie Holiday, Aretha Franklin, Pete Seeger, and Bob Dylan—signed Springsteen to a solo contract with Columbia Records. Within a month, Springsteen had recorded his first album, *Greetings from Asbury Park, N.J.*, which Columbia scheduled for release in January 1973.

Unusually for him, Springsteen had written the lyrics of the songs for *Greetings* first; only after the verses had been completed did he sit at his secondhand piano and attempt to set them to music. Never before had he written songs this way, nor would he ever do so again.

Given this technique, it is no surprise that *Greetings* seems so centered on (some might say weighed down by) its lyrics. The record's first song, "Blinded by the Light," explodes in a torrent of excess verbiage and (barely) postadolescent bravado. It crams an amazing 514 words into just over five minutes, one triple-rhyming line following another in a mad cavalcade of "drummers, bummers, and Indians in the summer," all intent on dethroning Dictaphones, hitting them in their funny bones, because "that's where they expect it least." "Blinded by the Light" is, no doubt, a twisted autobiography, with Bruce himself the "teenage diplomat / In the dumps with the mumps"—written with only his own youthful memories (and, he admitted later, a rhyming dictionary) to guide him.[4]

But where the lyrics of "Blinded by the Light" are so idiosyncratic as to be pretty much incomprehensible without a line-by-line analysis by the author himself,[5] Springsteen's next song, "Growin' Up," presents a universal portrait of adolescent angst and cussedness with which all but the most severely straight-edged and straightlaced might identify. The process of growing up is a finely balanced dance, Springsteen reminds us. On the one hand, there is an intense need to fit in and find our place in the "clouded wrath," "clouded warmth," and "mother breast of the crowd." On the other hand, adolescence is all but defined by its mandate to rebel—to strike forth on one's own—and to differentiate oneself from that same crowd. It is that time when, indeed, we are expected to "break all the rules" and yearn for the chance (at least in our fantasies) to strafe our own high schools, never once giving thought to landing back in the fields of normalcy and conformity.

Springsteen certainly is singing a young man's song here (he was, after all, only twenty-three years old when *Greeting from Asbury Park, N.J.* was released). But there is nothing puerile about Springsteen's innocence on this record (if innocence it be). It is more the "innocence" of a child growing up in a war zone, perhaps, than of a protected and coddled middle-class American adolescent. One senses that already Springsteen sees the world with eyes open wide to the truth and that he carries within him a wisdom beyond his years. His portrayal of teen angst is as far removed from the common domesticated variety as the real Freehold of his youth ("one of the skuzziest, most useless and plain uninteresting sections of Jersey," in Lester Bang's turn of phrase)[6] was from the bland Ozzie-and-Harriet vision he grew up with on the television screen. The young man's heart may yearn to head for "where the fun is" (as in "Blinded by the Light"). But the adult within knows that a far rougher world is never more than a city block—or the next song on the album—away.

New York City—bursting with energy and excitement as it does—might seem the perfect antidote to life in a place (like Freehold) where nothing ever seems to happen. To Springsteen, the heart of the city beats with passion and an irresistible call of life. In the song "It's Hard to Be a Saint in the City," he presents a stunning portrait of himself as a young tough announcing his arrival on the streets of New York: "I had skin like leather and the diamond-hard look of a cobra," he sings. "I was born blue and weathered, but I burst like a supernova." The scruffy, awkward, always ignored outsider from out in the sticks has arrived to claim his rightful place as prince and prophet at the very center of the world.

But while the city promises much, the price it exacts is great. Often, Springsteen knows, the city's call is one of a devious siren and not a blessed summoner. "The devil appeared like Jesus through the steam in the street," he sings. The vision of the streets turns out to be not an apparition of holiness and goodness but of deceit and evil. There is the lure of money and power—but to be gained only through the sacrifice of one's own honesty and integrity. It is, certainly, a tough choice for a "boy out on the street" to make.

But it is a choice that people in the city—and by extension, modern society in general—are called upon to make constantly. Some have already been defeated in this constant struggle to maintain one's integrity in the face of the alienation and dehumanization of urban life. Some, like the "sages of the subway," are now little more than "living dead"; others are still holding on, but only "by just a thread." Still others face a day in, day out battle not to be devoured by the frenetic pace of modern life, which roars ahead like a subway car speeding along the tracks at breakneck speed. At all costs, they must avoid the city's life-crushing underworld, which runs like a sweltering, stifling tunnel beneath the surface of everyday life. As the young Springsteen already understood, for so many men and women, the great challenges of modern life don't revolve around sainthood, but sheer survival.

Ceremonies of Innocence Are Drowned

Often in the background of *Greetings from Asbury Park, N.J.* is the war in Vietnam. Springsteen himself had avoided the draft when he flunked his physical exam in the summer of 1969. But even though he hadn't been sent to fight, many of his friends from high school had. At least one—Bart Haynes, who had played drums in the Castiles—had not come home. "And the guys that did come back were not the same," Springsteen later told *Rolling Stone*.[7]

For these Vietnam veterans, there would be no sweet homecoming, no heroes' welcome. For too many, there was merely the exchange of a foreign, physical battlefield for an internal, psychological one. For them, the war still raged; its wounds still burned. Even though the July 1970 ad for one of Asbury Park's music clubs had implored would-be patrons to "forget about the war" and come to the coast and party, Springsteen couldn't forget.[8] The violence and mayhem that was erupting on the streets of America's cities (including his own) seemed but an image and likeness of the violence still continuing in the jungles of Southeast Asia.

Perhaps the most intense song on *Greetings from Asbury Park, N.J.* is "Lost in the Flood," where plenty of blood flows and war imagery rages through every verse, and where the connection between the external war being fought overseas and the internal one raging in the American soul is drawn clearly.

In the song, a no-longer-innocent Vietnam veteran returns home not as a shining exemplar of American manhood, but as a "ragamuffin gunner"—not like a hero, but "like a hungry runaway." What he finds back in the U.S.A.—this cradle of liberty and freedom he has sworn to defend—is no better than what he left in the jungles of 'Nam. Indeed, both countrysides—domestic and foreign—are in flames. The two meld and merge in his mind in one inseparable vision of a second coming—or a second fall of humanity—as haunted as anything in William Butler Yeats's "Turning and turning in the widening gyre." Perversion is rampant. All have lost their convictions. Even the most sacred vows lie broken and discarded, as "nuns run bald through Vatican halls pregnant, pleadin' immaculate conception." Everyone is implicated and no one is safe. We're all "wrecked on Main Street," poisoned in our dens of (supposed) innocence and security. We're all "drinking unholy blood"—taking part in a dark and debased Communion—sharing a poisoned cup that promises not a new covenant and new life, but only despair and degeneracy, murder and mayhem.

Through all this intense—some might say overwrought— imagery of the endtimes, Springsteen presents his vision of an earth that is fallen and a world that has gone mad. The war has devoured all. Whatever hopes of domestic bliss and a Great Society that might have existed have now imploded. The holy is debased. Genuine relationships lie ruined. Communication is impossible, and no one can understand what anyone else is saying. When the shooting finally stops, nothing abides but "junk all across the horizon," like so much discarded military hardware.

The carnage of Vietnam has become the carnage of America—truly, of the whole world. One desolate landscape becomes indistinguishable from another. Just as America in the early 1970s stood lost in the flood of an irrational and ill-conceived war, so we all stand lost in the raging torrents of an unforgiving, merciless life, which sooner or later drowns all of us in its wake.

Loves and Lives Lost

Springsteen may have been an extremely young man as he wrote and recorded *Greetings*, but as "Lost in the Flood" illustrates, he had already, apparently, seen enough of life—and of love—not to romanticize it unduly. Even the seemingly buoyant and upbeat "Does This Bus Stop at 82nd Street?"—a pleasant enough romp through Manhattan's Upper West Side—talks about disappointed aspirations and the ambiguity of life in the city. The driver of the bus calls the neighborhood children by pet names—but also has an aversion toward people who walk with canes. He has his prejudices too. Dock workers and Black Panthers might be scheming to "someday own the rodeo"—but odds are, in the racially charged atmosphere of the times, they're not talking to each other. Sexual merchandising might be everywhere, with "tainted women in Vistavision" performing "for out-of-state kids at the late show." But none of this does any good for poor Rex, who's been "left . . . limp" in the throes of sexual dysfunction.

By the end of the ride, a young girl named Mary Lou can still affirm that "the dope's that there's still hope," with plenty of good, decent, hard-working people all around. Nonetheless, life in the city still counsels caution, as the "lucky young matador" will understand when he discovers that the precious gift thrown his way by "Spanish Rose" is not a prized blossom but an old, used Kleenex.

Likewise, there is a certain amount of sexual tension, if not downright dysfunction again, permeating the ponderous "The Angel," as well as the equally turgid "Mary Queen of Arkansas." In the former, the protagonist seems more lustily engaged with his car (his "hunk metal whore") than with the real flesh and blood (and underaged) female ("Madison Avenue's claim to fame") who stands seductively before him.

In "Mary Queen of Arkansas" there is also plenty of sexual imagery, and we can assume that the relationship here has at least been consummated. But something is missing. Mary is not "woman enough for kissing," the singer states; she holds him tight but loves him "so damn loose." Death imagery is everywhere: there are gallows waiting for martyrs, and the "shadow of a noose" hangs over Mary's bed. It all sounds more like preparations for a funeral than a romantic tumble, with a dirgelike, solo acoustic accompaniment thrown in for good measure.

The depth of the relationship between sex and death is examined much more passionately in "For You." Here the romantic relationship comes to a tragic end when one of the partners commits suicide. In more recent years, Springsteen has said that "For You" was "his first attempt at a love song,"[9] and the song is full of details of the topsy-turvy life this man and woman had together. Indeed, as Dave Marsh has written, as the song (and the life of one of the protagonists) ebbs, "we come to know both characters with a startling degree of intimacy, and to grasp the dimensions of their relationship."[10] In "For You" Springsteen is honing his skill as a keen observer of details, as an artist able to guide his listeners toward coming to know his characters as real people, as fully fleshed-out, living—or in this case, dying—women or men.

"For You" is a song about love, as well as a song about death, and Springsteen here sings passionately about both of these fundamental realities. The first verse alternates between happy memories and sad ones: there is an irresistible Cheshire smile, beckoning with its charm and mystery, but there are also those "barroom eyes" that shine like a vacancy sign—obscuring the spirit that dwells within this wounded, tortured soul.

By the second verse, matters have reached a critical stage—the point from which there will be no return. The singer is in the ambulance with his girlfriend on the way to Bellevue Hospital on Manhattan's East Side. As he looks down at her on the stretcher, more memories—more like a list of past battles—flood though his mind.

Here before him is a lover who has tormented him time and again—for whom he has come to the rescue over and over—around whom he has centered his life, with little, if any, apparent payback. But now, the thought of losing her leaves him utterly frantic. "Your life was one long emergency," the chorus sings, with the exasperation of one who has failed repeatedly to exorcise the demons of someone he has loved. Finally, he reaches the sad conclusion that there is nothing else he can do. "It's not your lungs this time," he tells his dying lover, "it's your heart that holds your fate." But apparently her heart has already been shattered too extensively for it ever to be repaired. She has given up on this life, slipped this earthly coil, and "left to find a better reason than the one we were living for."

An Earthly Hope

"I have found life an enjoyable, enchanting, active, and sometime terrifying experience, and I've enjoyed it completely," the great Irish playwright Sean O'Casey wrote in his memoirs. "A lament in one ear, maybe, but always a song in the other."[11] Such might well be an appropriate summation of *Greetings from Asbury Park, N.J.* Certainly, the album's songs present a rather tortured landscape of fear, dysfunction, temptation, suicide, war, and senseless violence. In Springsteen's view, the world is an imperfect, fallen place, and hardly a romantic paradise. Nonetheless, the album bursts with energy and the uncontrolled exuberance of youth. It seems to "laugh and cry in a single sound," as the singer in "For You" tells his self-destructive lover.

Life wounds us over and over again and gives us plenty of reasons (and opportunities) to cry and to sing that sad lament. But often, too, life also rings with the magic of laughter and of hope. There may well be great pain at the heart of life, but there is great joy there as well. Sometimes drawing the boundaries between the two is difficult, and if it is our fellow human beings who cause most of our pain, so it is also they who bring us most of our joy.

"Spirit in the Night" is the song that gives *Greetings from*

Asbury Park, N.J. its heart. While Springsteen's classic statement of adolescent bravado, "Growin' Up," already had a bittersweet air of nostalgia about it, "Spirit in the Night" seems anchored in a living present. It attempts to freeze that perfect moment when life is all of a piece and everything is as it ought to be.

Of course, on a purely historical and physical level, that night at Greasy Lake will turn out to be as fleeting and transient as any other episode in the lives of the song's main characters. But on a deeper, spiritual level, that holy night will abide forever. It is now locked away in the sacred vault of memory, which nothing that happens to these five people over the next ten, twenty, thirty, forty, or fifty years will be able to destroy. With "Spirit in the Night," Springsteen has, for the first time, left the mean streets of the material world and started down the enchanted pathway of myth.

But it is an enchanted pathway affixed firmly in the tangible details of the physical world. Forty years before Springsteen, the Irish poet William Butler Yeats's Crazy Jane had complained to her bishop (her "mission man" as it were) that "Love has pitched his mansion in / The place of excrement." But in Springsteen, no such dichotomy of the physical and spiritual worlds is drawn. In his vision, the physical world serves as a bridge to the spiritual, precisely because it is so accessible to the senses, so tangible, so damned real. There is nothing theoretical or merely intellectual about the caring and love these characters have for one another. As Dave Marsh rightly points out, "The key word in the final chorus ('Together we moved like spirits in the night') is 'together.' "[12] Together, Janey, Davey, Billy, and Joe—the characters in "Spirit in the Night"—form community; together, they provide for one another some earthly hope.

Even the mythological land of Greasy Lake, with its soul fairies and gypsy angels, isn't perfect—or, at least, it can't be permanent. One senses that when the bright stars and shining moonlight fade away, the enchanted spirit of the night will give way to the mundane and boring light of day. Already, even as Crazy Janey and her man sanctify the earth with their lovemaking and sing their "birthday songs" in celebration of life, there are signs that the world, and its troubles, is drawing in too close already. The world is already too much with Killer Joe, and he has "passed out on the lawn." Hazy Davy is hurt, too, delirious from inhaling (or, more likely, imbibing) too much freedom, perhaps.

With the rising of the sun, sacred night will be forced to yield, and the playful "stoned mud fight" of Billy and Davy down by the edge of these enchanted waters will give way to the real battles and casualties of the world as it is. Escaping the world is not the same as transcending it. Usually the world finds some way of snaring us back in. But sometimes, in our bold attempt at escape, we capture just a momentary glimpse of what transcendence might really be. So, too, our earthly loves—the friendships we share, the communities we build—can give us just a glimpse of heavenlike glory.

Chapter Two

Creating Community
The Wild, the Innocent, and the E Street Shuffle

*S*parks fly on E Street when the boy prophets walk it handsome and hot."

So exploded the opening lyrics of Springsteen's second album. But sales for *Greetings from Asbury Park, N.J.* were creating no sparks in the music world, certainly. Initial sales were disappointing and radio airplay insignificant. Among critics, however, *Greetings* had been at least a modest success, with many commentators intrigued by the imaginative verbal banter of this "new Dylan" from the Jersey Shore.

Almost immediately after the release of *Greetings* in 1973, Springsteen set to work on a follow-up—hell-bent, it seems, on avoiding some of the mistakes of his first effort. Most significantly of all, perhaps, Springsteen chafed under the burden of the "new Dylan" label. While the 1960s folk music revival, including the early work of Bob Dylan, had certainly had an influence on him, other forces were at least as important in his musical development: Elvis, Buddy Holly, Chuck Berry, Roy Orbison, among other early rock and roll pioneers; the "king of soul," Sam Cooke; and the Beatles, whose pioneering influence on popular culture no budding musician living through the 1960s could be free of.

Gone from Springsteen's subsequent work would be the self-conscious wordplay that had largely characterized *Greetings from Asbury Park*. While the lyrics of his new songs could not be characterized as spare, words alone would never again come to dominate an album as they had in his first effort. (Indeed, his second album would be released with no lyrics at all printed on the jacket sleeve—making the point that Springsteen was a musician first and not someone interested in emulating the "poetics" of Dylan. Given Springsteen's sometimes garbled articulation, many fans would have to wait over two decades—until the publication of the printed version of Springsteen's *Songs* in 1998—to figure out exactly what he was singing back in 1973!)

The spare, acoustical settings of *Greetings* had been something of an aberration for Springsteen as well. After all, he had made his name as a rock and roll musician, not as a folk singer, and had always performed as part of a band. "For this [second] record," he wrote later, "I was determined to call on my songwriting ability and my bar band experience."[1] He wanted to communicate some of the "physicality" that had always characterized his club-based music.

That meant solidifying his band. For this second album, it would have five members, in addition to Springsteen: Vini "Mad Dog" Lopez was on drums, Springsteen's old friend Danny Federici played the accordion, Garry W. Tallent was on bass (and tuba), Clarence Clemens—known as "Nick" back then—played the saxophone and contributed background vocals, and David L. Sancious handled keyboards. Bruce himself played all guitars, harmonica, mandolin, and recorder, as well as doing lead vocals on all numbers. Together these six musicians set out to realize Springsteen's vision of a much larger work than *Greetings* had been: a well-developed record album, almost operatic in its scope and tone, which would recognize rock and roll's debt to jazz, blues, Latin music, and soul. Springsteen himself had christened the group the "E Street Band," reflecting the E Street address of David Sancious's mother in Belmar, New Jersey, where the band originally practiced.[2]

The Great Dance of Life

Bruce Springsteen released his second album, *The Wild, the Innocent, and the E Street Shuffle*, on September 11, 1973. In a sense, it didn't seem as though he had traveled very far. The locale was pretty much the same, as was the atmosphere it exuded. The songs were still centered in life on the Jersey Shore, taking occasional forays into New York City. The first song that bursts forth, "The E Street Shuffle," is set along the streets of those weathered (if not beaten) beach towns along the New Jersey coast. In these songs, too, Springsteen's characters still seem to be direct reflections of people he had known in Asbury Park and its environs over the years.

But from the album's opening notes, we sense that something has changed. Gone is the lonely strumming of the solo guitar we had become used to hearing on *Greetings*. Instead, we are greeted with the slightly jarring tones of a group of musicians finally coming to find their groove. Gone, too, we sense, is the barely-past-adolescence brooding of Springsteen's first work. It is as though ten years has passed, rather than ten months. The characters on *The Wild, the Innocent, and the E Street Shuffle* are older and wiser than their earlier counterparts. They are now too busy searching for community and connection to sit home alone dwelling in a pit of prolonged introspection. It is still hard to be a saint in the city. But now Springsteen realizes that even a "boy out on the streets" need not dance alone.

"The E Street Shuffle," then, issues its invitation to everyone listening to join the dance. "Everybody form a line," Little Angel, Power Thirteen's girlfriend, sings in the chorus, over and over. "I wanted to invent a dance with no exact steps," Springsteen said. "It was just the dance you did every day and every night to get by."[3] There are no set steps and no limitation to who can join; the only criterion for membership is to be listening to the song—to *be awake* to the vibrancy of life.

"The E Street Shuffle" is a celebration of this earthly, earthy life in its most embodied forms, and sexual imagery is rampant. "All the little girls' souls go weak," we hear, when "the man-child gives them a double shot." We can imagine what "all the stops" the schoolboy pulls out on a Friday night really are. Dancing on E Street is about moving one's body in work, in play—and yes, in sex—in order to get in touch with one's real self. Joining the dance means forging community with all those around you; it also means accepting the challenges and complications that connection will bring.

Certainly, things aren't perfect on E Street (or in the world, which is E Street writ large, after all). The threat of violence, and the loss and anger and self-destruction it inevitably engenders, is ever present. Some haven't joined the dance yet; they're still "hooked up in a scuffle"—at war with one another, at war with themselves. Many still dance steps that are all too tentative. But in the E Street vision at least, "sweet summer nights" of bodies joined, and friends together, and connections made can give way at last to never-ending "summer dreams" where everything is loose and lazy and "all the kids are dancin' " a vibrant dance of life. This is a universal dance that excludes no one and in which all are brothers and sisters in a community as wide and open and free as the whole world.

"The E Street Shuffle" presents a vision of acceptance and inclusivity from which Bruce Springsteen has never strayed very far.

The Challenge of Change

Before the realization of any vision, however, there lies the vast expanse of the world as it is: a world with its full share of heartache and pain. "All life is suffering," the Buddha taught: not because we human ones are intrinsically evil, or because of the entry of some malevolent force onto the scene, or because the gods choose to torment us, or because of some great cosmological fistfight between good and evil. Life is suffering simply because everything in life is transitory and impermanent, and life at its most basic tends inevitably toward decline and decay and passing away.

This is our great human dilemma and the root cause of so much of our suffering. We know that everything is passing away, but this does not stop us from clinging to the people, places, and things around us nonetheless. We want them to abide forever, even though we understand full well that they cannot. The living moment cannot be bottled up or preserved, and even the sweetest hours of our lives hold within them the seeds of their own demise.

The song "Fourth of July Asbury Park (Sandy)" seemingly opens in the midst of one of these sweetest hours. It's the Fourth of July, and fireworks gild the sky over the ocean, illuminating the beach and the intent spectators below. "Switchblade lovers"—fast, shiny, and sharp—cruise the main streets of town, while elsewhere bare-chested "boys from the casino" cavort around "like Latin lovers on the shore." It is a sensuous and idyllic vision, and for everyone, it seems, there abides the promise of "this boardwalk life"—an endless summer, with its uncomplicated amusements, undemanding relationships, and promiscuous sex.

But soon we come to understand that the idyll is passing away. Soon the novelty of a life that is all freedom loses its allure; we grow tired of the shallow enjoyment of "bangin' them pleasure machines," whether of the mechanical or human sort. Like the singer in this song, we get stuck on a tilt-a-whirl—trapped in a life that keeps us spinning and spinning in the tedium of mere existence on the exterior of things.

Soon the pace of change and decay accelerates, and before long even the old constants of life aren't consistent anymore: a love cools and a relationship dies; the object of our ardor goes off with someone else. Even Madame Marie, the fortune teller, source of all wisdom and all knowledge, is closed down by the police, for the powers of this world have no place for mysticism, and mystery, and abiding wonder.

This "boardwalk life" is dying, as certainly as any earthly notions of eternal summer, perennial youth, and life without pain and challenge. The illusion has ended, and while in the end the singer promises his everlasting love, his voice quivers with uncertainty and questioning, and he knows that only the reality of the present passing moment truly abides.

This sense of inevitable loss can instill within us a deep fatalism and a feeling of helplessness. "Ooh, what can I do?" the singer repeatedly mourns on "Kitty's Back," the album's next song. Sometimes the challenges of life seem so large that all we can do is shrug our shoulders, fold our hands, and lament continually, "Ooh, what can I do?"

Kitty, we are told, left to "marry some top cat." She turned her back on her community, traded it in for life in the big city, and ran away with some bigwig supposedly so much "better" than the people around her. But it didn't work out. Now she's back, more as a ghost from the past than a promised savior, perhaps. Poor Cat, her jilted boyfriend, who knows that she's been untrue, seems to have no option open to him but to take her back.

But as he sings plaintively, "Ooh, what can I do?" one senses within him little hope for any positive change. Often in life there is a sense of movement, even of drama, as when Kitty returns to the alley. The train keeps moving down the tracks; the river flows inexorably on. But oftentimes life's just a tilt-a-whirl that keeps us spinning and spinning, returning time and again to where we started. Some highways lead down dead-ends; oftentimes the communities we escape *to* are as dysfunctional as the places we come *from*.

The myth used to be, of course, that every young boy dreamt of running off and joining the circus. Of course, this was more common when circuses weren't just playing huge arenas in major cities but would travel across the country every summer, pitching their tents in communities all across America. One place they stopped every summer was Freehold, New Jersey, Springsteen's hometown.

The circus, with its sense of exoticism and mystery and the parallel community it represented, appealed to Springsteen from an early age. He remembered the strange array of characters that would appear in town every summer, and, as he grew older and took to the road, he was struck by how much the itinerant life he had chosen for himself resembled that of a circus.[4] "Wild Billy's Circus Story" is his attempt to plumb a little more deeply some of these early memories. In it, Springsteen presents a remarkably vivid cast of characters, each one with unique talents, and each one tormented by some particular affliction, addiction, or imperfection. Indeed, as we look closer at the circus, we soon come to see that it is no more sacrosanct—and no less rife with irony—than the everyday world most of us inhabit. The machinist may look "like a brave" as he climbs the Ferris wheel; he probably just thinks he has to tighten a bolt somewhere. The mighty fire eater—the one for whom shooting flames bring no fear—has been downed by the heat wave as surely as anyone else. The man-beast in his cage salivates over a bag of popcorn, hardly a carnivore's delight. And the finger-licking midget is about to be taught a lesson in table manners by the humungous fat lady, Missy Bimbo. Even under the Big Top, there is about to be a rather harsh fall to earth—quite literally—for one of the Flying Zambinis, who is about to miss his fall, as the ring-master exclaims in shock, "Oh God save the human cannonball."

Just as Kitty couldn't find love in the city and had to return to her old neighborhood, so Wild Billy finds no joy in being a circus clown. He packs his bag and makes plans to escape back down the highway of his disappointed hopes to the small Ohio town from where he came.

We can't go looking for people and places outside of ourselves to bring us bliss, Springsteen seems to be saying. The place where we dwell might change. We can run off to the most exotic or urbane surroundings imaginable. But if we are empty inside to begin with, we will find only a desert there when we arrive. Unless we bring our own love, and joy, and hope to what we experience in life, we are not going to find those things anywhere else.

The Fallen City

Just as he did on his first album, Springsteen leaves the Jersey Shore for a time and, once again, heads for New York. But here, too, his tone has changed and his perspective has deepened. Springsteen's tales of the city in this second album are drawn in greater detail and with greater skill, as he starts to hint unmistakably at his profound talent as a storyteller. There is in *The Wild, the Innocent, and The E Street Shuffle* more of a sense of characters who are real people, and not simply generic types, or even carica-tures. The loves of these new characters seem to run deeper and from more genuine streams; for that reason, their falls, when they inevitably come, seem all the harder.

Because they are drawn in more vivid hues, we have more of a sense here of people who are *experiencing* life more deeply and authentically. Whether or not they are enjoying it more, or receiv-ing more from it, remains to be seen. Indeed, often their occasional joys and victories seem wrested in spite of the world, and not because of it. Oftentimes these joys burst forth exuberantly onto the scene, only to give way in time to a pervading sense of acquiescence. The city in Springsteen breathes a certain air of melancholy, as though his characters sense that their short-lived triumphs are often just the bridge to inevitable defeat. Whatever their outward self-confidence, they understand that they hold no special position of power or privilege, and so they may be forgiven for doubting in the end if the world really is a very friendly place.

To Springsteen, the heart of the city beats with passion and an irresistible call of life. But often, he knows, that call is one of a Siren, and the result of answering it can be brokenness and despair. As exciting and alive as the city seems, it is no less fallen than the rest of the world—and because of the intensity of life as it is lived there, disappointments seem all the more disheartening, like the breaking of some greater promise.

The song "Incident on 57th Street" begins with a series of melodic notes on the piano, which soon open up to the deep tones of an organ and lush, romantic guitar strumming. It is a romantic, almost symphonic introduction to Gotham. But first impressions are often deceiving, and things are not always what they seem—especially in the city, with its deep layers of affectation and its constant rebuilding and redefining of itself, which often hide what was really there in the first place. Springsteen may liken Spanish Johnny to a "cool Romeo," and Puerto Rican Jane to a "late Juliet," but we know what happened to the original Romeo and Juliet. There is no real reason to suppose that the fate of these two modern lovers will be any better.

Once the lush musical introduction gives way, we hear that Johnny has arrived and that he is "dressed like dynamite." Actually, of course, he is bruised and broken, arriving in town in a beat-up old car. He has arrived back in a place where love has been debased, where hearts "fall apart so easy," where "hearts these days are cheap."

We also become privy to a good deal of romantic banter that goes on in the relationship of Johnny and Jane, and we know that these are two people who care deeply about one another. But one also senses that threats of disloyalty, violence, and loss are never far removed from the surface. Whatever their talk of future meetings on Lover's Lane and of walking toward the sunrise together, these are people just hanging on to the twilight of their youth, with their best years already behind them. Even Johnny admits to the children on his doorstep that summer may be long, but "it ain't very sweet around here anymore." Finally, the all-knowing sister, the local nun—who, from her lofty and transcendent perch truly discerns what's going on—breaks down and weeps in the chapel when she's alone. No doubt, she knows that these kind summer spirits, however romantic and aspiring their hopes, are more likely than not doomed to join the ranks of lost souls. Such is the way of this nontranscendent, material, urban world where temptation breathes in every moment and the beautiful and the sinister are so closely intertwined.

In "New York City Serenade," a song with a very similar theme to "Incident," Diamond Jackie and Billy have taken the places of Jane and Johnny. Their hopes, too, seem to lie in escaping the city—this "mad dog's promenade," as one of them labels it. Diamond Jackie "won't take the train," Springsteen sings. She knows that the city and its restrictions—its tracking us blindly toward what is "expected" of any of us, given our particular stations in life—offers no hope of redemption. Nor does she want to lead a passive life of joining the jazz man's serenade of depression and despair. "Any deeper blue and you're playin' in your grave," Jackie tells the "vibes man." "Save your notes," she tells him. Don't waste your talent and treasure on despair, she infers; spend your money for the enjoyment of life; save your music to sing a victorious song of life.

But where will this victory be found? By listening to "your junk man," as Johnny, a drug pusher himself, insistently suggests? Such would seem a surer route to perdition than to paradise. Certainly, Johnny seems confident enough. Last time we hear of him in "Serenade" he's "all dressed up in satin, walkin' past the alley." He cuts a fine figure, at first glance, at least. Perhaps he wears the satin of a shiny new pimp's suit; perhaps he's just coddled in the satin lining of his casket. We're told that he's heading "straight for the church"—with the pride of one, perhaps, headed directly for his own funeral? Whichever way he's headed, the road he now walks (or is being carried down) is a dead end. "He's singin', singin', singin' ," we're told. But is there any reason to believe that the real song that lies beneath this deceptively lush and melodic harmony is not, in truth, a funeral dirge?

Finally, Always, Rosalita

For many Springsteen fans, it always came down to Rosalita. For over ten years between 1974 and 1984, during the most formative portion of Springsteen's career, "Rosalita (Come Out Tonight)" was featured in every show he and the E Street Band played. Usually, it was the very last number before the encore. But by the late 1980s, "Rosalita" had become a rarity; by 1990, it had disappeared entirely from the set lists for Springsteen's concerts. (Springsteen's hard-core fans issued a collective gasp of hope when the band finally performed the song in all its glory at the fifteenth of the sold-out shows at the Meadowlands arena in East Rutherford, New Jersey, that launched his Reunion Tour with the E Street Band in the summer of 1999. Banners imploring Springsteen to "Sing Rosalita!" were draped over the balcony of one concert venue after another. A steady murmur making the same request would usher forth from the crowd, night after night, city after city. Alas, Bruce heeded his fans' entreaties for their favorite song barely a handful of times over the next two years. During the 2002–2003 tour, however, "Rosalita" was back as a nightly fixture on the Springsteen set list, and longtime fans greeted the return of "Rosie" like the restoration of a dethroned monarch.)[5]

To be sure, a large part of the song's appeal can be explained by its exuberant and untrammeled musicality. The song had been written by Springsteen as a show-stopper, and it certainly was all of that. In his nightly renditions of "Rosalita" in those early years of his career, all the physicality of Springsteen's live performances exploded with full force. He would jump up on the piano, dive into the audience, be dragged away by screaming female fans. In the nine or so minutes he spent singing (and dramatizing) this one song, Springsteen seemed intent on capturing all of the uncontrollable energy of youth.

There were deeper reasons for fans bonding with "Rosalita" as well. A clear identification was established between singer and song, and bonding with Rosie meant, for many, bonding with Bruce. Many fans seemed to feel that in paying tribute to this one song, they honored and affirmed this most esteemed performer as well. Moreover, in paying homage to his (realized) dreams, they honored their own (often unrealized ones) too. Springsteen himself, after all, had called this song his "musical autobiography." "I wrote it as a kiss-off to everybody who counted you out, put you down, or decided you weren't good enough," he said.[6]

"Rosalita" was Springsteen's declaration that he *was* good enough—and so was Rosie, and so is any one of us when we remain true to those people and those things we love and dare to break free from a life that has grown too small to hold us any longer. "Rosalita" was his declaration that the old yardsticks for measuring "success" or "achievement" just aren't valid anymore.

This song is the ideal summation of *The Wild, the Innocent, and the E Street Shuffle,* because it brings together with such self-confidence and sincerity the record's three stated components of wildness, innocence, and community. "Rosalita" calls upon its listeners to dare to be wild, to sail those "pathless and wild seas" of life, as Walt Whitman (another son of New Jersey) put it. It honors also the innocence within us, which dares to reach out and love another, and dares even to declare and exult in our love. Finally, the song invites us to dance together with one another again and again and again, until the very crack of dawn.

"Spread out now, Rosie," the singer commands at the song's start. It's an invitation to open up sexually, perhaps, but it is so much more. Our hero has come to perform surgery on the woman he loves and to cut the umbilical cord that ties her to her family and their limited vision of what life can be. He's going to "cut loose her mama's reins," he says. He tells her not to hide any longer but to join him out on the road to liberation as, together with all of their free-spirited friends, they "make that highway run."

Where are they headed? "I ain't here for business," the singer says. "I'm only here for fun." He's inviting her to join him in a place where the expectations of the world are turned on their heads, where what's important are not the dreary, gray affairs of business as usual but, rather, the call of bliss and the profession of joy. "We're gonna play some pool, skip some school, act real cool," he tells her. They're going to "stay out all night," he says. They're going to abandon all the have-to's and ought-to's of the "adult" world (a world that seems to promise them nothing but tepid relationships and stultifying boredom and alienation). They're choosing instead a (seemingly) more innocent world of friendship and passion and romantic love, a world where they can be both wild and innocent at the same time. This new life beckons as close at hand as the front door of her house, the singer tells Rosalita. Go through that door, he implores. Get out of that stultifying prison of a household. Free yourself. Nothing holds you back but your own lack of will.

"Rosalita" is, of course, a song of youthful bravado. But even here, Springsteen holds open his hands to those who might oppose him. No branch is severed from the tree of life—not even the branches holding Rosie's (or his) boring and unimaginative parents. Springsteen understands the perspective of the "adult world"—of Rosie's parents—even as he knows they must leave it behind if he and his beloved are to have a chance at a fuller, freer life. He sympathizes with these adult figures, but he knows he can never be like them—not if he is going to be true to himself.

But then, when all hope of reconciliation seems lost and communication has broken down (and Rosie's sad, and her mama's mad, and her papa has locked her in her room), the means of redemption and even a sort of reconciliation appears, like manna from heaven. "Tell him this is his last chance to get his daughter in a fine romance," Springsteen announces. He has just gotten a "big advance" from a record company!

Springsteen may not want to be part of the world wrought by his father, or by Rosie's. But he knows how to speak a language they will understand. It's a language of dollars and cents, perhaps, but it's also a language that demands that even dreams prove their worth in what they produce—in what they achieve—in the workaday, real world. Through this curious and lively mixture of youthful wildness and hopeful innocence, Springsteen has maintained his integrity, proven his love, and has even found a job that pays!

Of course, it's only a matter of time before the veneer is torn from this wild, innocent youth. Youth cannot last forever. Even the guitar players who strum all night and all day—and those who dance to the music they hear—will grow old and tired eventually and will have to stop playing and dancing. Sooner or later, even their energy will dissipate. But even in remembering our youth, we store away just a bit of that energy to helps us get through our later days.

In the midst of all the crises facing Rosalita and her mother and father, Springsteen reminds her that "someday we'll look back on this and it will all seem funny." It is a line that seems trite, almost inane, at first hearing. But there is great wisdom in those words. "Time, like an ever rolling stream, bears all its sons away," the eighteenth-century hymnist Isaac Watts wrote. But there is a healing power in time as well, which Springsteen hints at here. Time bears much away—every one of us eventually and all that we love. But time also has this way of providing us with perspective and showing us the real gravity (or lack thereof) of many of those matters we trouble ourselves with, which seem so very important as we're living through them.

The importance of these "big deals" is often just an illusion—an illusion the flowing current of the years washes away. What abides then is the clarity and care with which we have touched others and, perhaps, the fleeting steps we have taught to others as they shuffled with us through the dances of our lives.

Chapter Three

A Romantic Rhapsody

Born to Run

On the night of May 9, 1974, Springsteen and his band opened for Bonnie Raitt at the Harvard Square Theater in Cambridge, Massachusetts. In the audience was Jon Landau, a music critic for the alternative weekly *The Real Paper.* Two weeks later, a long rambling reminiscence by Landau appeared under the title "Growing Young with Rock and Roll." Toward the end, it contained one of the most famous (some would say prophetic) lines in the history of rock criticism: "I saw rock and roll future," Landau enthused, "and its name is Bruce Springsteen."[1]

In spite of having spent almost a decade in the music business, having two critically acclaimed record albums on a national label, and having a hard-core fan base stretching farther and farther down the Atlantic seaboard, Springsteen was hardly a household name. Even in the wake of Landau's rave, commercial success still eluded him. Both *Greetings from Asbury Park, N.J.* and *The Wild, The Innocent, and The E Street Shuffle* had been disappointing sellers. There were rumors that some people at Columbia Records were planning on dropping Springsteen if sales on his third album didn't show a marked improvement. Springsteen's entire income for 1973 had amounted to the princely sum of five thousand dollars.[2] The next year, spurred by slightly better sales on the second album and a nonstop touring regimen that had the band playing more than 125 shows during 1974,[3] income for Bruce, manager Mike Appel, and the five other members of the band had picked up somewhat—to $8,500 each.[4] But the E Streeters were hardly on Easy Street: creditors constantly nagged Appel for past due payments, rent on his New York office consistently ran two months or more in arrears, and one day in Ohio early in 1974, saxophonist Clarence Clemons had been taken away in handcuffs because Appel had failed to send in a child support payment to Clemons's ex-wife.[5] Clearly, there was a lot riding on this third album.

Though he hardly disparaged the lure of commercial success, Springsteen was looking for something more than a Top 40 hit. This was to be an album, he hoped, that would capture the very essence of the rock and roll myth, that would clearly reflect its hope and promise and capture something of the glory, transcendence, and redemption rock and roll claimed to offer.

The vehicle of transcendence would be, more often than not, a car. Not since Kerouac had a spokesman of American popular culture so clearly recognized the significance of the automobile as a deep icon of our national spirit. The album's ethos—its defining motto—would be captured in the phrase "born to run." Springsteen himself later recounted the origins of the propitious phrase:

> One day [in, perhaps, 1974 or so] I was playing my guitar on the edge of my bed, working on some song ideas, and the words "born to run" came into my head. At first I thought it was the name of a movie or something I'd seen on a car spinning around the Circuit [in Asbury Park], but I couldn't be certain. I liked the phrase because it suggested a cinematic drama I thought would work with the music I was hearing in my head.[6]

In this work Springsteen would create an epic of life in this "runaway American dream"—an epic populated by normal, everyday people to be sure, but in which these normal folk would appear consistently larger than life, almost mythic, and in which all of their day-to-day endeavors would come to symbolize deeper spiritual and emotional struggles.

While not a concept album per se, *Born to Run* is nevertheless cinematic in its scope; there is both a dramatic progression from scene to scene (or song to song), as well as an internal cohesion between the different songs. While the songs differ widely from one another stylistically, and while there is little (if any) overlap of characters from song to song, there is a sense nonetheless that all of the songs here are of a piece, and that they belong together. Springsteen himself has suggested that it might be helpful to see all of the events on the album occurring in different locations, over one "endless summer night."[7] What we have here, then, from the first strains of "Thunder Road" to the final notes of "Jungleland," is Springsteen's view of a "day in the life" of America, both at its harshest and most dangerous and at its most energetic and hopeful.

We Can Make It if We Run

"Thunder Road" sets the scene for the journey. Spare notes from Springsteen's harmonica, gently echoed by Roy Bittan on piano, evoke an almost bucolic scene: a rural tableau of sunrise over a split-rail fence perhaps, maybe even with a rooster crowing in the background. It seems at first a strikingly rural locale for a young tough like Springsteen, who once prided himself for being "just a boy out on the street." As the album begins, we seem to be smack-dab in the middle of the American heartland—a place of screen doors slamming and women's dresses billowing and waving in the wind, and long conversations on the front porch. We're a long way here from the Jersey Shore or New York, certainly, with their own icons of busy streets and subways and manic activity.

But even without these familiar touchstones, we soon feel as at home here as we would on any city street. The journey that these characters in "Thunder Road" take is the same that we will see later on the album, when we return to those more familiar urban settings. The same specters haunt them; the same hopes light their days and fire their nights. With *Born to Run,* Springsteen takes another step toward universalizing his narrative. His concern is no longer merely with people like himself—those who are perennially scruffy, angry, skirting the line of the law, if not completely over it, and unapologetically urban (though hardly urbane). By locating "Thunder Road" off in the boondocks somewhere, Springsteen pays deeper homage to the challenges and trials of everyday, working Americans who are not "like him" (at least out-wardly). We may no longer be in the heart of the city, but we are still in the heart of the human predicament.

The narrator here is imploring his girl, Mary, to take a chance on the next stage of her (or their) life. "Thunder Road" is a song about graduation, about commencement, about getting on with the next stage of life, about hurtling forward into the future—for only in the future can the promise of a more abundant life be redeemed.

As we listen at first, "Thunder Road" might seem like just another love ditty, just one more romantic tête-à-tête. Mary comes out onto the porch to meet her man, who issues what seems like a typical, plaintive plea. Don't leave me, he begs; I don't want to be alone anymore. When he pleads with her not to run back inside, we might be forgiven in thinking that this is a rather garden variety domestic drama unfolding before our eyes.

But soon we realize that Mary is not being beckoned to the young man's *back seat*, with all of the predictable messiness that back seats connote. Rather, he's calling her "from your front porch to my front seat." She's not being beckoned to as just another girl to be used and abused and then discarded, but as an equal on the journey. Here, at last, we sense that this road trip might really be different, that it might not be the same old dysfunctional journey Mary, or those like her, have made so many times in the past.

But Mary isn't sure that she wants to come along. Who can blame her? It's a frightening thing to start down a whole new road, to graduate to a new stage in our lives. The what-ifs keep flashing in our minds; we keep hearing those voices (inside ourselves, and perhaps from the people all around us) that keep telling us that we'll never make it. "Maybe we're not that young anymore," the singer acknowledges—to which we can each add qualifiers of our own: Maybe we're too old, or too young. Maybe we're too fat, or too slim. Too underqualified, or too overqualified. Too gay, or too straight. Too poor, or too rich. There are any number of ways we can find to tell ourselves that we're just not good enough. We don't quite measure up. We have to do more, and do it better, to be wor-thy enough to reach out and grasp that for which we truly yearn.

But other voices call out to us too. These are the voices of those who believe in us, those who really care. There is also a deep, inner voice that reminds us of how strong and how brave we can be.

"Show a little faith," the singer implores, because "there's magic in the night." The future glows with possibility. There's something magical in our dreams. There's magic in the creative powers of our minds and imaginations and intuitions. "There are divine things well enveloped," Walt Whitman said. "There are things more amazing than words can tell." There's magic in that deeper vision of who we can be.

But how do we realize this hope, and kindle these flames, and glorify life and the Creator of life? Certainly not by dwelling in the past—in past hurt and past pain, or even in past glories and accomplishments. Nothing will change if we "hide 'neath [our] covers" and cling to the ways the world has hurt us. Nothing will change if we luxuriate in the mere memory of past triumphs and past conquests, clinging to loves and lovers already dead and gone. Nothing will change if we put all our hopes for salvation outside of ourselves—if we waste the whole summer waiting "for a savior to rise from these streets." If we keep waiting for someone else to rescue us and save us from the dead-end streets and high brick walls we come upon in life, and never take the next step for ourselves, then nothing will change.

Life only changes, and progresses, and improves, when we accept life, as imperfect as it is, and find some way to build upon it. We may not be heroes or beauties, but we don't have to be either to live out life fully. So very often we have been blessed in life by people who have held us close, and have loved us, and have believed in us—in spite of how unheroic or unbeautiful we may have been. As the poet Adrienne Rich said, there will always be those among whom we can weep and still be counted as warriors. There are always those among whom we can fail and still be counted as victors.

We may never measure up to the standards of success our culture sets, and in the glare of celebrity, the common light each of us possesses might seem small and very dim. But when Springsteen sings that "all redemption [he] can offer . . . is beneath this dirty hood," he is saying that our real salvation doesn't lie "out there" in the demands of church or state or society. Real salvation is inside, right here—beneath *our* hoods—under our chests, within our hearts, beating steadily in the engines of our souls. A heart that beats true and faithful and hopeful energizes and inspires and motivates a life that is open to its deepest possibilities. Even if our lives may seem outwardly unremarkable, we may well have remarkable journeys yet to make.

So, the narrator tells Mary, it's time to *live*, before you die inside. Before the dreariness and the boredom get the best of you and kill all that is creative and growing within you, just get in the car, hit the road, and "let the wind blow back your hair."

When they are fueled by the magic of hope, and empowered by the light of dreams, then these paths we trod (or drive) day in and day out can have all of heaven in them that we'll ever need. Our own "two lanes"—the way of life that is ours to live—"will take us anywhere," even to that heaven that is "waiting on down the tracks." Time is fleeting, and the years of any of us may well come too quickly to an end. We don't get an unlimited number of tries to "make it real," and the ride is never free, and there will be promises that we will have to break, and once-upon-a-time lovers we will need to send away, and there will always be so much letting go in this life.

For all of us who are alive there will be those times on the cusp between darkness and daylight when we look most deeply into our souls. They are the times when we will feel most alone and, paradoxically, most at one with all that is. Here, "in the lonely cool before dawn," we hear all that we have ever known of security and predictability receding further and further away into the night. We may even glimpse again apparitions from our past: ghosts that do not necessarily haunt or engender fear anymore but that can no longer be part of who we are. Once the energy of the present, living moment has left them, phantoms of the past become mere carcasses along the road of life, "skeleton frames of burned out Chevrolets," with no power or drive left in them.

At this time of great transition, we might well feel most unsure of ourselves, uncertain that we have made the right choice. But once we are committed to change, the darkness breaks, and morning with its immense possibilities finally arrives. The only choice we have, then, is either to remain here in this "town full of losers"—here among the ranks of those lost souls whose best years are already behind them, who have not responded to the call of life—or to move forward and become one of those living, breathing, fully human beings, intent on exploring the possibilities life holds, casing the promised land, and "pulling out of here to win."

Companions on the Journey

Bruce Springsteen is much too keen an observer of the great procession of humanity in its wide array to rely exclusively (or even predominantly) upon the facts of his own autobiography for inspiration. However, Springsteen is hardly a mere innocent bystander when it comes to this wondrous human pageant, and we have seen, even in the days before fame and fortune exploded over him, how his life epic had its own share of both drama and comedy.

Certainly, there are times when Springsteen's own personal experience lies very close to the meaning of his work, and the autobiographical nature of a particular song is unmistakable. One such song is "Tenth Avenue Freeze-Out," a stylized, even somewhat mythologized version of the formation of the E Street Band.

As the song opens, there are "teardrops on the city" and things are looking glum, because "Bad Scooter" (note the initials) is struggling to find himself as a musician. He feels hemmed in ("can't find the room to move"); he's in a rut; his back is "to the wall" (as Springsteen himself felt up against the wall, facing the make or break pressures of his third album). Scooter's life might seem bleak (his "night is dark"), but life is going on all around him; the streets of the city are "lined with the light of the living," and, as always, music fills the air.

But Scooter is unable to respond to life. He's walked into a "Tenth Avenue freeze-out": Even in the midst of this life all around—in the very heart of the city—he feels frozen out, "all alone," cut off from his home and the things that once motivated and stimulated him.

Then, at last, prayers are answered, and a change is made "uptown." Maybe the source of this change is uptown in Harlem, where a new musician for the band is found. Maybe the source is *way* "uptown"—indeed, heavenly—and the hand of grace has decided it is not good for Scooter to be alone and so has beckoned comrades and friends to share this earthly coil with him. Either way, everything changes when the Big Man joins the band: the ice is shattered and the once-frozen waters begin to flow again. Bad Scooter finds his groove. Destiny beckons, and Scooter and the Big Man stride forward to meet their day.

We just can't do it alone. "We are caught in an inescapable network of mutuality, tied in a single garment of destiny," Martin Luther King wrote in his famous "Letter from Birmingham Jail." Meeting destiny is a collective endeavor, and we are defined, if not totally then at least to a predominant degree, by our relationships. We would not be alive without them, and we would not know our place in the world (and be able to find our groove) if it were not for our sharing of this life with others.

Sometimes, as in the case of the Big Man—Clarence Clemons—joining the E Street Band, these relationships encourage us, bring us great joy, and make us smile, sigh, and say, "Life is good." At other times, our relationships challenge us, stretch us, and even well-near kill us. "Life sucks," we may then complain, and then gird ourselves for the next round.

Sometimes, in spite of all voices of reason and common sense and much evidence to the contrary, we pursue those relationships we ought not to. Some people entice us, with their beauty, or their charm, their wit, their intelligence, their sense of exoticism or mystery. As with the main character in "She's the One," theirs is the smile that kills us; theirs is the particular array of attributes—lips, hair, eyes, being—that summon us forth unto them, even unto what we know might well be an unhappy end.

There are some "secret places" in the souls of others we will never be able to fill. There are "hearts of stone" that all our passion and ardor will not soften, however deep our intimacy. Whatever their outer beauty, there are those who will never be able to "break on through" to their own inner beings. How then can we ever expect to join them there, or to join our being with theirs, if they are intent on remaining strangers to themselves? Yet we seem destined to try nonetheless.

"The secret is in your heart," the poet Brian Andreas tells us. "Of course," he then adds, "knowing that doesn't make it any easier." There are those relationships that are doomed to bring us only pain. But it is the pain of one who refuses to turn his or her back on life.

Escape to the Backstreets

Life is worthwhile precisely because there are others who *do* allow us to touch their souls—in friendships so deep that we almost seem to share a single soul at times. But in order to "break on through to the inside"—the place where all real relating occurs and all deeper living takes place—we need to escape, at least for a time, the nine-to-five world of our daily responsibilities and the expectations that world has of us.

As Springsteen's song "Night" implies, escaping the world of daytime, with the whirr of its machinery and its garish lights and its incessant noise and chatter, may be the only way for the gentle and sensitive souls of this world to survive spiritually, and perhaps even physically in some cases. "Night" is a great anthem in praise of "the close and holy darkness," as Dylan Thomas described it.

The workaday daytime represents a living death for too many people, during which they seem to be responding to ringing bells like Pavlov's dogs. The ringing bell of the alarm clock wakes them up, and they spend the rest of the day passively answering the call of authorities outside themselves. On the other hand, it is the night that "feels right." The night, with the world "busting at its seams," seems unable to contain the energy and brilliance of its dreams and possibilities. "Soul crusaders"—men and women determined to live from the deepest imperatives of their souls—have crowded the streets. They answer neither to bell nor boss but only to that deeper call of life. This is what it means, Springsteen says, really to *feel* alive, to feel as though "every muscle in your body sings." So it is to be truly in love with life and "in love with all the wonder" that life brings.

"Night" is that time when we dare to hold close and honor all of that which is hidden and mystical. Darkness brings relief from the blinding sun, from scorching heat, from exhausting labor. Night signals permission to us to rest, to come home, to be with those we love, to conceive new life, to search our hearts, and to remember our dreams. Night can be that time our deeper thoughts and inspirations have the chance to grow in the dark and fertile ground. "Night" is not a particular hour of the day so much as it is a deeper state of mind.

The song "Backstreets" also reminds us that we are born as children of the holy fire, children of the Spirit. But the ways of the world often separate us from our blazing birthright. To find enlightenment and passion again, we must escape the world and head for the desert, for the outskirts, for that place away—in this song, an "old abandoned beach house."

Once again, the workaday daytime is a mere prelude to the holy night for which we wait expectantly. The call to life—"the bells that ring in the deep heart of the night"—free us from everything, or at least from everything that doesn't matter. Answering that call frees us to go out and rekindle "the fire we [were] born in" and to answer creativity's summons.

But even along the backstreets, the world is never far from us, and it puts up an awesome struggle to exert its control. Even the backstreets are littered with those who attempted to escape the world but were pushed back down. We see their broken and maimed bodies; we hear their anguished cries. Sooner or later, we find that, so very often, "we're just like all the rest"; we're not heroic at all, or at least not heroic enough to transcend the world indefinitely. In the depths of the night, we perceive how truly tragic life is, and we discern how exhausting and futile constant resistance against life's realities can be. So, at midnight, as yet another overpowering day beckons, "the breakdown" comes. We surrender to the light of day, under whose intense glow the sins of the world lie exposed in all their corruption and brutality. All that then abides are the sad and angry memories of broken oaths, faded friendships, and dissipated passions.

Whatever its deep sense of pathos and yearning, "Backstreets" is, ultimately, a tragic song, and one can hear the genuine regret in Springsteen's voice as he sings it. As Dave Marsh describes it, "[Springsteen] sings 'Backstreets' with true grief, so mournful that he seems ready to swallow the whole world for solace." [8]

A Runaway American Dream

There is no guarantee that our journeys will end heroically. But "Born to Run" is a defiant anthem that offers at least the joy and exuberance of the search, if not the certainty of final victory. The song itself is a musical tour de force that took Springsteen and his band more than six months of intense effort to record.[9] From Ernest "Boom" Carter's intensive drumming at the beginning, through an incessant array of guitars layering their notes one upon another, over a roaring wall of sound, pierced occasionally by a manic saxophone riff, "Born to Run" races through its four-and-a-half minutes like one of the "suicide machines" springing forth onto the highway of which it sings. The song never lets up, never looks back, and, for most of Springsteen's fans, never grows old.

Once again, the setting of the song is at night, in that place beyond polite society and the world's expectations and demands. But unlike "Backstreets," where the goal seemed to be some kind of heroic transcendence of the ways of the world, the vision of "Born to Run" is founded solely on defiance. Its goal is escape for its own sake, and not for any higher or nobler purpose. The characters here are too world-weary to worry about anything besides escaping the boredom of the world before it brings them down. "We gotta get out while we're young," the narrator sings, " 'cause tramps like us, baby we were born to run."

The whole purpose of existence for these characters—their entire reason for being—is escape. No bright or grand or glorious destination beckons; no vision of a better world leads them farther on. Their goal is constant movement—trying something different and always new. Their creed, simply, is this: to "run till we drop" and "never go back."

Such might seem a rather limited scope for human endeavor. But it does offer the power and promise of the moment, well and fully lived. It also at least hints at a deeper yearning to know more and to understand more about life, The vision of "Born to Run" is hardly high and exalted, and its characters—its "tramps," as Springsteen labels them—are not in any way refined, idealized, or especially heroic. But they are completely human, and that is where their power and glory lies.

Indeed, when Springsteen addresses this anthem to all those "tramps like us," he's once again casting a wide-open, all-inclusive circle of people whose exterior circumstances in life might differ but who share both the deep scars and pains of life, as well as the deep yearning for a more transcendent life. Sprinsgteen's appeal to "tramps like us" celebrates our very human imperfectness. He doesn't sing out to "beautiful people like us" or "winners like us" or "cool cats like us"—that's not an accident. We're tramps, all of us. We're of the earth; we're a little dirty, perhaps; life has left us in disarray; we may even stink (on the inside, if not the outside). But in our comradeship with one another—our striving for community—we are fellow pilgrims in this journey through life. And that, at least, is worth celebrating.

There is a vibrant and vivid sensuality in "Born to Run" that celebrates life—and the sexual, embodied life at that. The idea of wrapping our legs around another person's "velvet rims" or strapping our hands across someone else's "engines" bursts with a sense of sexuality still in its prime. But it is a sensuality that, while definitely physical, never deteriorates into the carnal or exploitive. While we might assume that the kids who are "huddled on the beach in the mist," are hardly chaste, there seems something almost innocent and protective of one another in their lovemaking. Likewise, there is something ennobling in the desire to die with one we're with out on the street, locked in an "everlasting kiss"—as though life itself is finally sealed and redeemed in the kiss of an eternal youthfulness and a love of life that will never fade or die.

Even here, on this endless cruise around town—this journey without a destination—a sense that we might be looking for something deeper, something more after all, rears its head from time to time. "I want to know if love is wild," the singer explodes. "I want to know if love is real." It's not enough for him, apparently, that love is exciting and physically satisfying; it needs to be "wild" and "real" as well. It has to be a genuine plant, with roots deep in the heart of the beloved, bringing forth a burgeoning flower of true ecstasy and passion. No window box variety of love will do, nor one confined by the tepid limitations and expectations of society, nor one offering a merely mechanistic and purely physical approach to lovemaking. A real love—a wild love—is somehow *more* than physical. It points toward the spiritual, toward a deeper communion of one person with another.

This place out on the horizon (that place where some day we'll "walk in the sun") is where all this "running" is headed: a vague, ultimately unknowable place where we break out of the endless cycle of circling the block—the endless cycle of dead-end jobs, relationships that don't last, and friendships that fade away, that place where sadness is no more, love is real and wild and unlimited, and all is one. The characters in "Born to Run" probably don't have a clue how to "get to that place where [they] really want to go." Furthermore, one senses that their endless circling and their incessant running won't, in and of itself, get them there. But even to yearn for heavenly bliss is to know at least a bit of its reality. And there is freedom, as well, in envisioning something more heavenly than this sadly deficient world as it is.

What's Flesh and What's Fantasy

The *Born to Run* day that began so promisingly so long ago and so far away on Thunder Road is now drawing to a close. Night has fallen and we are back in the city. The characters here seem more like those of Springsteen's earlier, Jersey-based work: there's Eddie, a girl named Cherry, and a narrator who seems a hopeless screw-up, the kind of guy desperate enough for quick cash that he would pawn his girlfriend's radio. Whereas the tone of "Thunder Road" was one of hope and exuberance and morning in America, by the time we get to "Meeting Across the River" the tone is dark, and we're exhausted.[10]

"Born to Run" offered the bravado and defiance of characters set on taking a "last chance power drive." "Meeting Across the River" offers a much-less romanticized portrait of people who are down to their last chance, period. The narrator is appealing to his tag-along protégé, Eddie, for a few bucks, so they can get a ride "through the tunnel" for a meeting with "a man on the other side." They're headed for the other side of the Hudson River, certainly, but toward the other side of the law as well. The narrator also hopes that this "other side" offers a new opportunity to put past misfortunes and mistakes behind him.

We can sense the desperation in the narrator's voice, as Springsteen sings over a spare arrangement of piano punctuated by a trumpet's wail. "Word's been passed this is our last chance," the narrator sings. These characters are literally toeing a line of life or death—and all for a measly payoff of two thousand dollars (hardly a princely sum, even in 1975 dollars). That is how low their fortunes have fallen. One doesn't need to be a fortune teller to sense that things here aren't going to turn out well, however pompous the narrator's brag that "tonight we got style" and however vivid his imaginings of a happily-ever-after where he throws the money on the bed and goes "out walking." By the end of the song, after all the bravado, the high-sounding plans, and the imaginings of future bliss, the exhausted narrator is still plaintively begging a ride from his junior protégé—which is right where he began the song in the first place. "The other side" and all that it represents may beckon, but he has no idea whatsoever of how to get there.

Whatever the musical merits of "Meeting Across the River"— and in spite of its short length (only three minutes, eighteen seconds) and its being the closest thing *Born to Run* has to a throwaway—it continues to command its share of advocates among Springsteen fans. It was even the subject of an entire book written in 2005.[11] However, the song's chief purpose on *Born to Run* is to serve as a bridge from the exuberance and high spirits of "Born to Run" and "She's the One" to the introspection and heartrending passion of "Jungleland."

"Jungleland" is the classic culmination of *Born to Run*. From the delicate strains of Suki Lahav's violin at the start to the haunting vocal screams at the end, "Jungleland" portrays an epic battle between forces of innocence and forces of experience.

At the beginning, as a piano tinkles merrily in the background, the forces of eternal youthfulness seem once again in ascendance: Magic Rat has pulled into town for a romantic rendezvous with his Barefoot Girl. But no sooner has their "stab at romance" commenced than the forces of authority and repression—represented by the Maximum Lawman—enter the scene.

"All is silence in the world," we are told, and the scent of confrontation is in the air. All across the urban landscape—"from the churches to the jails"—sides are chosen, and the battle begins. But in this fallen, blatantly unromantic, far-from-innocent world we inhabit, should there ever be any doubt about which side will emerge the victor? Already, as the sides are gathering, the powers that be are making steady, subtle inroads: the meeting takes place "'neath that giant Exxon sign"—a rather blatant symbol of the false "illumination" of a corporate, materialist mindset. In the "parking lot"—along the sidelines—in the abode of the masses, so-called visionaries are said to "dress in the latest rage," behavior about as revolutionary or countercultural as a trip to the mall. Girls who, supposedly, dwell on the backstreets are dancing to the Top 40 hits played by the mainstream DJ. From the get-go, there already seems too much compromise with the world here for any abiding victory over it to be achieved.

Still, the struggle persists. However outnumbered, the forces of fantasy and mystery forge ahead with their turnpike opera and their ballet in the alley. "Kids flash guitars just like switchblades," with a defiant insistence that creativity can conquer violence. Even the "hungry and the hunted"—those ignored or criminalized by the established order—"explode into rock and roll bands." They transform themselves into transcendent street gangs, insistent upon their message of passion and creativity.

But the real world is not a dream, nor does it care about transcendence or creativity or even passion. While lovers may find temporary salvation in one another's arms, and in the echoing rhythm of their beating hearts, out on the streets a far harsher reality holds sway. Uptown, the Rat is gunned down—but at least he had a dream. For the most part, the world at large seems like the girl in the song who turns out the bedroom light. She is lost in her own little concerns; she doesn't even know that there's a great struggle going on just outside her window.

In "Jungleland" a battle rages to determine what kind of world we will inhabit. It is a battle between forces of violence and materialism on the one hand, and those of creativity and transcendence on the other: "between what's flesh and what's fantasy," in Bruce's resonant phrase.

This material world is, as Wordsworth wrote, "too much with us." It has become a junglelike land of getting and spending, and winners and losers, and survival of the fittest. It is far from the Edenic garden we dream the world could be. It is far removed, too, from the boundless hopes and wide-open highways of "Thunder Road" with which we launched *Born to Run*'s endless summer night. Now, finally, the night has drawn to a melancholy close, back on the streets of the city. Once again, ceremonies of innocence seem to have been drowned.

Even the battle cry of this great conflict fails to move most of us beyond the boundaries of our little lives. Either paralyzed by fear or sated by our small pleasures, most of us stand back like voiceless poets, inspired by nothing, writing nothing, doing nothing. Then, when it's already too late, we reach for our moment; we "try to make an honest stand." But the moment that called for heroic action, when our sacrifice might have planted seeds of change, has already passed us by. So we end up wounded by the ways of the world but offering no real challenge to its iniquity.

Springsteen's great scream that ends "Jungleland" is as different from the gentle violin strains at the beginning of the song as two pieces of music could be. Indeed, that scream contains all the pent-up rage and frustration that Springsteen could muster, aimed at a world where too many dreams lie broken and abandoned. But with all its anger, fatigue, and dread, the very vitality of that scream is also evidence that while those dreams may have been deferred, they are not dead. There is defiance, and not just exhaustion, in Springsteen's voice here: the defiance of one who has learned his lesson, who has let go of shallow innocence and affected naiveté and who truly understands, at last, just how challenging and demanding—yet nerve-rackingly real and alive—this world can be.

Chapter Four

Maintaining Integrity
Darkness on the Edge of Town

The commercial success of *Born to Run* decisively routed any movement at Columbia Records to dump Springsteen. By the end of 1975, just a few months after its release, the album had already sold over 900,000 copies.[1] If Bruce Springsteen was not yet a household name, he did at least seem well on the road toward becoming one. His concerts had been well-attended, from Providence to Seattle (and in places like Iowa City and Omaha in between). Reviews of his third album had been almost universally complimentary. Typical among them was that by Greil Marcus in *Rolling Stone,* which characterized the work as "a magnificent album that pays off on every bet ever placed on Bruce Springsteen."[2] Overnight, it seemed, Springsteen had been transformed from a northeastern cult figure into a genuine national celebrity. The hype over *Born to Run* reached its apogee in October 1975 when Springsteen became one of the very few people ever to be featured on the cover of both *Newsweek* and *Time* in the exact same week.

However, Springsteen's relationship with his manager, Mike Appel, was steadily deteriorating. The original contract Springsteen had signed back in 1972 had given Appel a sizeable portion of the revenue generated by his work, as well as full publishing rights over all of his songs. Intense and involved wrangling over matters of fiduciary control only aggravated growing creative tensions between the two, with Appel advocating more explicitly commercial endeavors, which Springsteen continued to resist in the name of artistic integrity. Finally, in July 1976, about a year after the release of *Born to Run,* Springsteen fired Mike Appel, accusing him of mismanagement. Appel, in turn, countersued Springsteen, charging him with breach of contract. As a result of this power struggle, Springsteen was barred by court order from recording with his new manager, Jon Landau (the same Jon Landau who had called Springsteen "rock and roll future" and the man often credited with the overwhelming artistic and commercial success of *Born to Run).*

We can only take Springsteen at his word that "The Promise," a hauntingly reflective song that debuted and was featured prominently in Springsteen's concerts during this period of strife, does *not* deal with his conflict with Appel. "I don't write songs about lawsuits," he told Dave Marsh in 1979.[3] Nonetheless, it is difficult not to perceive striking parallels.

The protagonist of "The Promise" seems mired in despair. He has a job but often skips work. Sometimes he just stays home; sometimes he goes to the drive-in movie theater. There he seeks to lose himself in celluloid fantasies that often work out better than real life does. Life, it seems, has foreclosed on his dreams. Crushed under a mountain of debts, he has been forced to sell his Challenger, the car he loves, which he built with his own hands. Control over his life has been surrendered to forces more powerful than he.

With nothing left to hope for, he is reduced to driving purposelessly to and fro down one dark, rain-soaked highway after another. He is emotionally dead—"dyin' on the highway tonight," as he puts it. He has come to view himself as little more than emotional roadkill along the way of life. He feels as though he is carrying all the sadness of the world on his shoulders—carrying "the broken spirits of all the other ones who lost"—of all those who have faced shattered loves or have been cheated out of their aspirations. But he carries these defeats with no sense of heroism, much less altruism. He holds no expectation that he can somehow redeem them. Life has weighed him down, and the burden he carries is, rather, like an albatross around his neck, a heavy weight in his soul, which he seems doomed to carry through all the days of his life.

As his legal struggle with Appel dragged on into 1977, Springsteen grew anxious and depressed and may have begun to doubt that he would ever make another record again. His career, if not finished, certainly faced a lofty barrier. Like the protagonist in "The Promise," he may well have felt that he had cashed in too many of his dreams.

Trouble in the Heartland

Finally, in the early morning hours of May 28, 1977, a settlement was reached. Under the agreement, Springsteen was released from his obligations to Mike Appel and was given creative control over his own music. In return, Appel was awarded an estimated $800,000 in cash and some small share of the royalties on the first three albums.[4]

Within weeks, Springsteen was back in the studio, recording his fourth album, with Jon Landau as producer. According to many people who observed Springsteen during this period, he approached his work now with a seriousness that bordered on stridency on times. It was as though having nearly lost "much of what [he] had worked for and accomplished,"[5] he now sensed the need for his work to stand for something more and the need to keep faith with all he had been through.

As soon as we hear the fourth album's opening words, we know that we are on a far different journey here than the romantic ramble that characterized much of *Born to Run*. The lights have gone out tonight, Springsteen sings in "Badlands"; there's "trouble in the heartland." From its very outset, *Darkness on the Edge of Town* is characterized by intensity and seriousness. The locale has changed, and we're smack-dab in the middle of the "heartland" now; we're no longer a boy out on the streets, or just a performer on stage, or a midnight rider cruising aimlessly around town. We've been hurled right into the thick of things, among real people, with their real lives, real responsibilities, and real tragedies.

With this fourth album, Springsteen wanted to show the world that he had grown up—and had grown not just older but wiser and more discerning as well. The last vestiges of adolescent bravado that clung to the edges of *Born to Run* have faded away completely. With *Darkness on the Edge of Town,* Springsteen found what he himself characterized as his "adult voice."[6]

America was changing, too, by the summer of 1977. The idealism of the 1960s was already a quickly receding memory. Instead, the 1970s had progressed through a messy withdrawal from Vietnam, the national trauma of Watergate, and a severely depressed economy. A new president, Jimmy Carter, had come into office in 1977 amid great plans and high hopes; but he, too, soon seemed overwhelmed by runaway inflation, soaring energy costs, and what came to be characterized as a growing "malaise" in the national spirit.

In "Badlands," when Springsteen sings "I want the heart, I want the soul, I want control right now," he represents all of those who feel themselves at the mercy of impersonal, spirit-crushing forces—all of those who are struggling to assert their personal autonomy and maintain their individual integrity in the face of strong forces of alienation and fragmentation.

This battle to survive—psychically and emotionally no less than physically and financially—is a constant struggle; indeed, we have to "live it every day." Sometimes its costs are unspeakably high and its casualties are numberless. But those costs—even the cost of a broken heart—is "the price you've gotta pay." This high cost is the emotional rent that we all are charged if we're to live authentic lives; it's the ownership fee that comes due every single day for the life that is ours to live.

When we pay this full price on our lives, and meet our obligations, and keep faith with those for whom we are responsible, then the remnant of hope abides, even in the midst of these badlands. Our reward for keeping faith and honoring our responsibilities is the hope that the tide may eventually turn and that a time may come when "these badlands start treating us good."

This is not merely some pie-in-the-sky, impossible dream of the poor man who fantasizes about winning the lottery and striking it rich. It is a much deeper and more genuine hope than that, because it is founded on bedrock values that emerge directly from real life and real relationships. "I believe in the love . . . in the faith . . . in the hope," Springsteen sings, as he invokes the three great theological virtues, one after another. It is these three—faith, hope, and love—that abide when all else is taken, as Paul reminds us in 1 Corinthians 13:13. In our living out of these virtues, we are raised above the muck and mire of these badlands toward a sense of life that is complete and whole.

When we live our lives honestly and faithfully, we "spit in the face" of those who deride our human race as hopelessly bound to sin and depravity (which is not to say that sin and depravity don't exist). As "Badlands" swells to its ultimate affirmation—"it ain't no sin to be glad you're alive"—we feel once again redeemed, whatever we have been through. We are ready to continue down life's road buoyed by our hard-won hope and with no little joy in our hearts.

The Working Life

Bruce Springsteen later said that after *Born to Run,* he "wanted to write about life in the close confines of the small towns I grew up in."[7] He seemed interested in exploring how—or perhaps, *whether*—the human spirit could flower from such arid soil and whether the human imagination could expand beyond such limited and self-limiting horizons.

While tremendous wealth was still years away for him (as late as the summer of 1976, Springsteen was taking home only $350 per week—the same as the other members of the E Street Band),[8] Springsteen could never forget his even more humble roots. It wasn't just a question of finally having more money; even more critically to him, he felt truly blessed to be able to pursue a career that fostered his spirit and creativity. In his music, he wanted to evoke those—like his father and mother and his friends back in Freehold—whose lives and aspirations had been much more severely circumscribed by the jobs they were required to do.

"Early in the morning factory whistle blows," Springsteen begins the lean and elegiac song "Factory"—in all, barely a dozen straightforward lines about "the working life" into which he had been born. It is that factory whistle—and not any profound inner voice, or creative muse, or deeper wellsprings of humanity or self-actualization—that will determine how these hard-working people will spend the hours of their days.

The whistle blows, and the man gets up and out of bed. Everything else he does seems almost predestined: as though programmed, the man gets his lunch, walks out into the early morning streets, and heads for the factory, always answering the relentless call of "the working, the working, just the working life."

Of course, such self-sublimation comes with a cost: physical (he's going deaf because of the noise of the machines) and emotional (the men who leave the factory at the end of the day have "death in their eyes," Springsteen sings, and their bottled-up rage against the machines, the monotony, the bosses, and the injustice of the system often explodes in domestic violence).

But just as the factory takes so much from this worker, so it also "gives him life." It provides him with a livelihood (paltry as it may be) and some sense of dignity and worth (fragile as that may be). Springsteen's "Factory" praises the unromanticized heroism of those who do what they have to in order to do their jobs, finish their work, and meet their responsibilities to those who depend on them.

But even as he understands the sacrifices his father has made, so Springsteen also knows that the safest road, often, is *out*. He may respect the life that has been willed to his father, but he knows that escaping from it provides his only chance to realize his own genuine dreams—not to mention to avoid his father's nightmares. Certainly, this escape is no simple matter, and it can be difficult to break out of the cycle of poor choices and unforgiven trespasses imparted from one generation to the next. In "Adam Raised a Cain" Springsteen seems to be echoing the God of the Old Testament who declares (Exod. 20:5; Deut. 5:9) that he is visiting the sins of the fathers upon subsequent generations. "You're born into this life paying for the sins of somebody else's past," Springsteen sings.

But such an obvious proponent of free will and personal responsibility as Bruce Springsteen could never cling tightly to any narrowly deterministic "birth is destiny" perspective. Rather, in his view, the interrelationship among past, present, and future is always more complicated than that, and the bonds that link the generations are neither static nor predetermined.

Certainly in "Adam Raised a Cain" we are presented with a vivid portrayal of father-son conflict. The father stands inside the doorway, the son is on the outside in the rain, and nowhere does there seem any hint of a spirit of unity bringing them together. Yet they are bound, father and son, as lovers and as prisoners—bound in a passionate love where that "same hot blood" that flows through their veins seems destined to percolate into nothing other than rage, regret, and blame.

It is a painful inheritance. But so vivid, so palpable—such a part of himself—is his father's pain that the son is able to know the power it holds over him. He has inherited his father's sins, certainly: the wrath, the envy, the pride. But he also affirms that with the sins "you inherit the flames"—the flames of his father's passions. Tragically, for the older one, the flame of life has often been extinguished by the pain of life. On those occasions when the flame was fanned into fire, it was invariably the fire of anger or rage or violence. But the younger one senses there can be more. The father lived "the dark heart of a dream," but at least he bequeathed a dream. It remains for the son to redeem their love and free it from the chains that have bound it to darkness.

He will do it by being true to who he is.

Something in the Night

Escaping the prisons of our fathers' and mothers' broken dreams is but the first step on the long road toward wholeness and integrity. We may have no sense of where we are headed, or who it is we want to be. The challenges may be awesome, and, as Springsteen sings in "Streets of Fire," often the place we find ourselves may be even more frightening and insidious than the place from where we have come. Or just more empty. The circumscribed former lives of mill, family, and neighborhood might have been small and oppressive, but at the least they offered honest work, a sense of purpose, and a modicum of community.

Now, with our backs turned on the past, the lights of the factory have been extinguished to us. Extinguished, too, is any sense of connection, any sense that we belong somewhere, or to someone. Now, in these bleak hours before we have remade our lives anew, it's as though all that could be taken from us has been taken. Our "eyes are tired" and we "don't care anymore." We want to let go of life itself; in truth, we probably would rather be dead. But we hold on, as much out of cold, frozen habit as out of any kind of conviction. We continue to wander through our days aimlessly, as self-described losers, while all about us the streets are on fire (again). But this time they burn not with a "real death waltz" toward nobility but with a hellish vision of anger, fear, and pain. Only strangers share this worldly hell with us—only people who don't understand us and whom we don't understand. Even the angels here on the streets (few as they probably are) are debased: they are "angels that have no place." They stand nowhere, so they stand for nothing; they are angels without any real faith, all-too-earthy counterfeits of heavenly beings. "Where there is no vision the people perish," says Proverbs 29:18. Where there is no purpose, life—however "free" of traditional cudgels it may be—will inevitably reflect more of hell than of heaven.

Sometimes, however, when we bid adieu to the old ways, we find that not everything is taken. Sometimes much abides; more often, all that remains is a simple sense of "something in the night" leading us further on. It is a great miracle of grace when this bare sense of "something more" is enough to sustain and nourish us as we continue down our road, and we finally discern that blessed "moment when the world seems right."

Oftentimes that blessed moment is a very long time in coming. Loss is an inevitable component of human life. "It can be said that only we human ones grieve," wrote the Unitarian minister Chadbourne Spring. "Only we lose a part of ourselves and feel the loss intensely. The more we feel, the more deeply we are involved in life, the more we grieve. . . . The only way to avoid grief is not to live. . . . Life means grief—in time. Love means grief—in time."9 Within this human life, it seems, someone is always demanding something of us. Somebody, somewhere, wants a piece of our time, our talent, or our treasure. "Soon as you've got something they send someone to try and take it away," Springsteen sings in "Something in the Night." It's tempting, then, simply to want to jettison all those needy relationships: the nagging spouse, the high-maintenance lover; the self-centered children. It's tempting to want to "take it all and throw it all away," as Springsteen sang in "The Promise."

But what is the result if we do so, if we jettison everyone and seek to go it alone? What do we become if we do, indeed, "ride this road till dawn, without another human being in sight"? In the very next line of the song, Springsteen answers the question: we become just another one of those "kids wasted on something in the night." We degenerate into an unformed, undefined, semi-human kind of creature, touching no one, caring for no one, existing from one fix to the next, from one cheap thrill to another.

A life without relationships is empty, Springsteen is telling us. But, of course, this is not to say that a fuller life—one that is moving toward completion and wholeness—is necessarily an *easier* one. None of us escapes from life without seeing some of the "things we loved . . . crushed and dying in the dirt." There is no escaping the pain that life brings, no chance at all that we will escape this life "without getting hurt."

Our wounds are reminders, though, of our humanity and our vulnerability. They are our badges of courage. The only way we come out of life unscarred is not to live—to turn our backs on life and give up our chase for that elusive, inspiring, life-sustaining "something in the night."

Hidden Worlds That Shine

Sometimes, after passing through dark and murky Hades, we cross over into our own golden, shining Elysium, with its offer of comfort and rest. As unheroic as we might feel ourselves to be, there will oftentimes be those who love us, who want to be with us, and who will, amazingly, choose to include us in their heroic pantheons.

"In Candy's Room" we hear that "there are pictures of her heroes on the wall." But it's not really these airbrushed heroes that Candy wants, nor is it the "strangers from the city" who bring her "toys"—baubles and trappings of a fake love and a debased relationship. She wants a lover who is real—whose smile is genuine, whose kisses are hot, and whose affections are not affectations. "What she wants is me," the singer states, in spite of his apparent scruffiness, lack of means, and inexperience. Candy wants him because he promises a deep sharing of bodies—but also something much more. It is because "Candy's boy" is so unaffected—so untutored to the ways of the world, still so potentially "wild"—that she believes him to be closer to that deeper love than all those "strangers from the city" who make their ways to her room.

What Candy wants from her lover—and what she offers to him in return—is a deep sharing of souls, and through that sharing a sense of transcendence. Their intense lovemaking becomes a hierophany: the means not only of knowing one another but also of knowing the Divine. Through our sexuality, we can transcend the limitations of this linear-rational, mundane existence and come to know some sense of union with the Absolute. We will glimpse those "hidden worlds that shine," and in the sharing of our bodies, we offer that sense of transcendence to one another.

As the theologian Dorothy Soelle has written, "Both religion and sexuality heal the split between ourselves and the universe. We discover that we are indeed 'part of everything' and one with the mystery of life. To talk about God in relation to our sexuality means to be aware of love moving in us, for 'in God we live and move and have our being.' "[10] Through our intimate sexual relationships we can receive—and offer—a deep and profound gift of grace.

None of this is automatic, of course. When we deal with the complex and fragile worlds of one another's psyches and souls, the field is laden with unintended consequences. "Life is what happens to you while you're busy making other plans," John Lennon once mused, and seldom do our lives conform to the scripts we may have prewritten for them in our minds. The true test of integrity, then, is to remain faithful to our lives when our plans lie shattered by the stern, unpredictable hand of real life.

At the outset of "Racing in the Street," the song's narrator seems to have it all together; in the object of his '69 Chevy he evokes a perfectly controlled universe. Not only does the car have every accoutrement one could want in such a vehicle, it has also been built *ex nihilo,* as it were—"straight out of scratch" by the owner himself, exactly to his own specifications.

With this perfect car, the narrator and his partner Sonny go from one town to another throughout the Northeast, drag racing the summer away. They are free of commitments and attachments, and victory comes easily. Theirs is an outwardly exciting life, certainly; they wander far from home. They refuse to imitate the small lives of so many of their contemporaries: working in the mill all day, following someone else's schedule and dictates, slowly "dying little by little, piece by piece" from the ennui and the boredom. Instead, when their work day is done, their real life—the life they spend racing in the street—begins.

But then everything changes. The once free and unattached narrator falls in love with a girl he spies in a Camaro with another street racer. He rescues the girl from the plastic, phony life of endless shopping malls and suburban sprawl, as together they drive away in his Chevy. But this is not going to be just another "guy gets girl" love ditty; there will be no simple and shallow happily-ever-after in this narrative.

Soon the haunting specter of despondency descends upon the girl, and in "Racing in the Street" Springsteen provides a harrowing portrait of the toll depression takes: The girl has grown old overnight, it seems; her eyes are ringed with deep circles as she "cries herself to sleep." She sits alone in a dark and empty house, or she spends her time just sitting on her father's porch staring into the darkness, "with the eyes of one who hates for just being born." This woman believes it is a sin for her to be alive. She has lost all faith in life and curses the very fact of her existence.

The narrator, on the other hand, continues to hope; he keeps on racing in the streets. But now he does it for some deeper purpose—as though to whisper in his lover's ear that life is still worth living. One night he will take her out of bed, or off the porch, and trundle her into the front seat of his sacred car. Together they will head for the sea—the great ocean of new possibilities—in whose life-giving waters the sins of the past are washed away and where new hopes for the future are born.

We don't know if there will be an upward trajectory in their life together. But we know, at least, that the girl will not have to face her demons alone. We know, too, that the once carefree racer has matured enough to trade his easy contests on the street for a much more challenging struggle.

Life's Full Spectrum

In *Darkness on the Edge of Town*, the wide romantic vistas of *Born to Run* give way to the stories of lives whose outward parameters seem so much smaller. Yet on *Darkness*, this sense of outward limits concentrates the reality of the situations with which we are presented. In "Prove It All Night," for example, the wide-open highway of which Springsteen often sang in the past has given way to a much more modest road: a short, insignificant trail out west somewhere, between two small towns—Monroe and Angeline.

In fact, it is along such relatively short highways that the lives of most of us play out their days. Most of us are not the movers and shakers of the world, neither presidents nor rock stars. We are simple men and women, most of us, in our day in–day out narratives; we are simple and straightforward, at least outwardly. We drive that familiar road (Monroe to Angeline; Westchester to Manhattan; home to work and back again; youth to old age to death) over and over. Sometimes its routine comforts us; just as often, perhaps, the daily sameness of it all becomes boring and drearily predictable. The ways of our lives offer their enticements, of course; their diversions and distractions, like the "gold ring and the pretty dress of blue" of which Springsteen sings in "Prove It All Night," give us some sense of color and excitement. But these distractions may not be enough to curb that deep inner yearning—the "hunger [we] can't resist"—because, unlike pie-in-the-sky, fairy tale dreams, these real lives of ours require something more substantial to feed them.

Life—even a simple, unremarkable life—costs so much more. When we really live it genuinely and fully, life sullies us and dirties our hands. As righteous and saintly as we think we are, truly living involves knowing what it means "to steal, to cheat, to lie." In the daily triumphs and tragedies of life, we learn what it truly entails "to live and die."

Life challenges us and compromises us, and the hand of life gives and takes away. But the gift of life is a divine and sublime gift, and in spite of everything, it is a gift for which most of us are profoundly grateful. By living our lives fully—and fully living the complete circle of good and evil, joy and sorrow that life is—we prove our loyalty to life, all night and all day, through all our days upon this earth.

By the time we reach "Darkness on the Edge of Town," the final song on Springsteen's fourth album, we might well feel bruised and battered. In these ten songs we've been through a lot together: broken families, shattered relationships, numbing jobs, depression and sadness, and the incessant demands of life. But, remarkably perhaps, we might feel strangely hopeful, as well—and thoroughly alive. In *Darkness on the Edge of Town,* we have been tried in the fierce crucible of life. And those who have not cracked have emerged all the stronger for it.

It is possible to skirt about life on the seemingly comfortable and prosperous surface of things, like the ex-girlfriend we meet at the start of the album's title song, with her big and stylish house in the fashionable part of the city. But style alone has little to do with inner worth. To live such a lukewarm and surface-dwelling life is not to know the liberating fire of the blood burning in your veins.

That feeling comes only when you face life head-on, accepting it in its full spectrum of light and dark. Life is stark at times, but it is also luminous with mystery. "Everybody's got a secret," Springsteen sings, "something they just can't face." According to the

Gospel of Thomas, if we liberate this deepest truth that is within us, it will free us; if we keep it hidden, it will destroy us. Similarly, in his 1996 book *The Soul's Code*, psychologist James Hillman developed what he called his "acorn theory" of the soul. According to Hillman, we each have within our psyches our *daimon*—the encapsulation of our soul's deepest potentialities. When we live life in connection with this *daimon,* we realize our destiny and answer our true calling.[11]

But this messy, earthly, earthy life often obscures our souls' secrets from us. We each may have a secret as Springsteen sings, or as Hillman theorizes, but just as often we remain secrets, even from ourselves. The convoluted ways of love and life, family and relationships, finding our place in the world, making a living, and getting along with others may seem the most inscrutable of mysteries to us at times. Much of who we are—and much of what life means—often seems hidden in darkness from us: a darkness on the edge of our realities, and a darkness on the edge of our souls.

We have been taught to fear the darkness. But perhaps by seeking to banish the darkness—by treating it as a sort of enemy and by refusing to embrace it and dwell within it fully—we have also banished an important part of our selfhood.

Be still. Go within. Listen to the holiness there. That's the message great mystics of various traditions through the ages have been imploring us to heed. That is the message this earth tries to teach us in the quiet of the night and in the stillness of winter.

Sometimes it is in the darkness that we see most clearly that which most needs to be seen. Sometimes it's out in the darkness on the edge of town—on the edge of existence—that we make the most important discoveries about who we are, where we've been, and where we ought to be headed next.

It is not always an easy trip, this journey we take, without or within. Pondering the darkness on the edge of our existence— looking within and really opening our eyes to what's there—means knowing ourselves, our whole selves, our true selves. For most of us, most of the time, this kind of intense self-knowing is just too painful. It is then that we feel ourselves in that place where everyone "looks too long in [our] face" and where, looking too long and too closely, they (and we) might even recognize the anger, jealousy, desire, fear, and remorse that dwell within.

So, like the ex-girlfriend at the start of the song, we run away from the darkness, back to the well-lighted, more "stylish" parts of town. We put on the lights, take a pill, have a drink, grab something to eat, get busy doing something, doing anything. We turn on the light so we need not see or feel what the darkness uncovers; we turn the radio up loud so we don't have to think.

But there are those brave enough to face the darkness within and the darkness without, to name what the darkness represents and what it offers. There are those of us—and there can be that part of each of us—who will "be on that hill" of self-knowledge whatever the cost, because we just "can't stop." We will be on that hill because we discern that unless we know these dark parts of ourselves too, and name them, we will not really know ourselves. And unless we know ourselves, and experience that deep sense of wholeness and integrity that self-knowledge engenders, then we know we will have no claim to that something deeper toward which our spirits yearn.

Chapter Five

Life Keeps On Rollin' Along

The River

*L*ike *Born to Run* before it, *Darkness on the Edge of Town* quickly went platinum: within four months of its release in June 1978, more than a million copies had been sold. Eventually, the album peaked at fifth place on the Billboard 200 chart for 1978. Sales figures for *Darkness* were impressive—just slightly below those of Springsteen's much-hyped magnum opus—though sales for both were dwarfed by the megasales of other albums of the times, including the Eagles' *Hotel California* (16 million copies in 1976), and *Rumours* by Fleetwood Mac (19 million copies in 1977), as well as by the best-selling album of 1978, the soundtrack to the movie *Saturday Night Fever,* which featured the Bee Gees and eventually sold over 15 million copies.[1]

But beyond the commercial realm, the growing force and power of Springsteen's public persona far transcended these decent-enough sales figures. He and the E Street Band were developing a reputation as the hottest live act in rock. They could sell out 10,000-seat concert venues more quickly and more often than those other performers who dominated record sales and FM-airplay.

A few months after the accident at Three Mile Island nuclear power plant in the spring of 1979, Springsteen accepted Jackson Browne's invitation to join an assorted group of antinuclear musicians for a series of four concerts at Madison Square Garden to benefit MUSE—Musicians United for Safe Energy. Springsteen, it seems, finally felt prepared to take a public stand

and put some political flesh on the social dissatisfaction of which he had often sung.

The MUSE sessions merely confirmed the growing strength of the "Bruce" phenomena. His participation guaranteed the fiscal solvency of the Garden concerts and the subsequent live record album that followed them. A constant murmur of "Bruuuce . . ." throughout the shows—whether or not Springsteen was on stage—served as a constant (and sometimes annoying) backdrop to all the other performers.[2] Kit Rachlis from the *Boston Phoenix* claimed that the response Bruce engendered as he came on stage for the first show was "the most frenzied" he had ever heard.[3] Even amid all those other stars from the rock and roll galaxy, it was Springsteen who seemed to glow just a little more brightly.

With the MUSE experience behind him, Springsteen and the band returned to the studio in the fall of 1979, to finalize, he hoped, work on his fifth album. They had already spent nearly six months recording, but much remained to be done, and the record's release would still be another year away. There was simply too much material from which to choose: well over twenty songs had been recorded, most of them album-quality or close to it. After his buoyant experience at Madison Square Garden, Springsteen also started thinking about including other works—songs that would give listeners a sense of the liveliness and exuberance of the E Street Band's in-person performances.

Now, however, Springsteen worried that the prospective album lacked focus: How could deep and pensive ballads about "real" people (similar to those that had characterized *Darkness*) exist on the same record with the raucous and upbeat rockers that distinguished the band's live performances? "I don't understand all these things," he ruminated. "I don't see where all these things fit. I don't see how all these things can work together."[4] Finally, after months of reflection, it occurred to him that maybe such inconsistency, representing as it did such a wide range of human experiences and emotions, was precisely the point. Life was all about living within the contradictions. "There's never any resolution," Springsteen said later, "there's never any making ends meet or finding any type of long-standing peace of mind about something."[5] In human experience, the moment of absolute certainty never arrives. There is never that point at which everything abides once and for all, all tied up in neat little packages, with all mysteries of the past, present, and future thoroughly explained away.

Life is never a calm and placid sea without ripples and contradictions, at least not for the long haul. More often, life is more akin to a great river that just keeps flowing along, bearing us all away in its current. So Springsteen's fifth album, *The River* (finally released in October 1980 as a two-record set), surges forth through twenty songs that differ widely from one another in content, tone, style, and scope. Sometimes the music wanders and meanders. It flows both fast and slow. It skims over shallows but then soon flows to a full and imponderable depth. At other times—as on the turgid and monotonous "Drive All Night"—it nearly seems to run dry.

You Can't Forsake the Ties That Bind

It seems entirely appropriate that Springsteen should begin this mammoth opus by exalting the importance of "The Ties That Bind" and reminding us of the overriding significance of our human connections to one another. Indeed, this is perhaps the narrative chord that connects the seemingly disparate songs on this big album. (It might even be argued that such is the narrative chord that connects much of Springsteen's work as a whole.)

Life is not always easy; even less often, perhaps, is it much fun. Sometimes we feel hurt and spent, to the point of being "all cried out." We feel angry to the point of wanting just to push everyone around us out of the way, as we tramp down the road of our own existence. To avoid the risk of entanglement, we build a wall: we act tough and cool out the outside in order to hide from the hurt we feel inside.

But pushing others out of the way alienates us from them; it breaks "the ties that bind." Human relating causes us pain—excruciating pain sometimes. But the alternative is the emptiness of a living death, the utter aloneness of having no one there to "ease [our] sadness" or "quiet [our] pain."

"It's a long dark highway and a thin white line" that connects us to one another, Springsteen sings. It's a perilous and precarious path that connects us to those we care about. The ties that bind are fragile and easily severed. But this connection—these paths of different lives joined as one—is the only road we have ultimately to make it back home to one another.

It need not be an odious journey. Even with all the hassles and challenges we face in our daily existences—like the pain-in-the-ass mother-in-law in the back seat in "Sherry Darling"—there's a lot to enjoy in life, a lot to cherish, and so much to love. "I got some beer and the highway's free," Bruce sings. "And I got you and baby you got me." It is the simple pleasures of our days that give life so much of its color and vibrancy. These simple pleasures bless us and grace our lives because they connect us ever more deeply to those we love. They are the fine threads from which are woven the bonds that unite us, one to another.

This makes the separation from those we love all the more poignant and, potentially, devastating. In "Jackson Cage," a man has been sentenced to life in prison. From his cell—his "cage"— he thinks of his woman (his wife perhaps) back at home and how her life, too, has been devastated by his incarceration and by their separation. All alone in the world, she too now faces a prisonlike existence. She has become "like the scenery in another man's play," without a life of her own that's worth living anymore. Just like her man in prison, she is doing her time and fading away a little more with the passing of each hard-edged day.

If we go on spending our lives playing "tough guy scenes" like some sort of Lone Ranger, then we do it at our own emotional, psychological, and perhaps even physical peril. "It is not good that the man should be alone," God declares in Genesis 2:18. Or, as Springsteen sings on *The River*, "Two hearts are better than one." Experience would seem to bear him out. For example, according to a recent clinical study cited in *Newsweek* magazine, people who think of themselves as lonely are more than twice as likely to get sick as people who don't. Moreover, the death rate among those with few personal relationships is three times that of people with numerous friends and relatives who live nearby.[6]

There is no peace of mind in being alone, Springsteen sings in "Two Hearts." Alone, the world turns "hard and cold" for us. It is in our search for our own "special one" that we experience a great part of life's brilliance and warmth.

Declaration of Independence

"Independence Day" is Springsteen's classic statement of father-son tension. Even before this song begins, apparently, a pitched battle has been raging. Now, as the hours drag on, both protagonists are exhausted; finally, the son tells his father to "go to bed." Having no doubt expounded their respective positions at great length (and perhaps with great passion and no little fury) nothing either one can say is going to change the mind of the other. The son is adamant: he will be leaving town the next morning.

But even before the end of the first verse, the tone of the song has turned from blame to compassion and from rebellion to understanding. The son isn't leaving in a fit of postadolescent pique, or because he hates his father personally. Rather, he needs to escape from the system and mentality that have crushed his father's spirit—and that now threatens to crush his own. "The darkness in this house has got the best of us," the young man sings. Indeed, their whole town now seems pervaded with this "darkness," this sense of dread, depression, and despondency. The son wants to get out before he ends up lifeless and empty too.

Like many fathers and sons, they have not grown up easily together. They have had their share of conflict—of choosing hurtful, harmful, angry words, and of drawing lines in the sand in defense of their own positions. But even at this late hour the son is able to see how much they have in common, how truly they are "too much of the same kind." He understands at last the import and depth of their shared history.

Now both face the relentless flow of time and the inexorability of change. "Life goes not backward, nor tarries with yesterday," Kahlil Gibran wrote. Life does not stand still; it keeps flowing and flowing (like a river). The old familiar haunts grow empty and close up shop; entire towns are rendered economically redundant; new people with strange customs and ideas move in.

One senses that the father in "Independence Day" is about to be swept beneath the river's rising current, if he hasn't been already. As the young man, his son, now prepares to leave town, he looks back in compassion and empathy toward his father and realizes, at last, how much the older man has been forced to surrender over the years. But he knows too that the dead must bury the dead. It is up to him now to point his own uncertain craft in the right direction—facing forward not backward, making change his ally and not his adversary.

There are shoals along the way, to be sure. An independent life can often be an aimless one—as Springsteen shows in the snappy "Hungry Heart" (his first Top 10 single). In spite of the song's infectiously up-tempo beat, the narrative of this three minute, nineteen second morality tale is bleak.

A man deserts his wife and children in Baltimore, leaving them high and dry when he goes out for a ride and never comes back. As he himself puts it, he's "a river that don't know where it's flowing," and, without the wise parameters of relationships and responsibilities, his life becomes a series of one wrong turn after another. To fill the emptiness in his "hungry heart," he falls in love (he says) with some floozy in a bar—a relationship he knows is doomed to fail from the start. Inevitably, after much drama and pathos no doubt, this relationship ends too, and the man is back where he started: all alone, still cruising aimlessly and looking to fill his needs without having to commit to something in return.

The shallow, uncommitted life can feel good, at times, as the outspoken sexual desire of both "Crush on You" and "You Can Look (But You Better Not Touch)" attests. But the self-mocking tone of both songs also seems to indicate that Springsteen understands that such freewheeling youthful bravado won't lead very far in the end.

But it is also true, of course, that the strongest interpersonal relationships can only be forged by those who have developed a healthy and secure sense of personal autonomy and self-esteem. The assertion of a strong sense of self does not preclude the ability to nurture resilient, mutually interdependent relationships with others.

"Out in the Street" is a fierce anthem in praise of self-expression. It asserts the ability of unremarkable individuals to transcend (at least temporarily) those impersonal forces that dominate their lives most of the time. The protagonist works five days a week, "loading crates down on the block." But when Friday arrives and his work week is over, his real self asserts itself. It is "out in the street"—in the world beyond the loading dock, and the factory assembly line, and the long lists of expectations piled on us by the powers that be—that the self finds its true home. When the self becomes fully alive, there is no more loneliness. There is no more feeling "sad or blue." There is then only a soul that dances and sings and a general air of benediction. "Baby, out in the street I just feel all right," the singer exults. Here, at last, he is living out the maxim of the church father Irenaeus, who said, "The glory of God is the human person fully alive."

The singer knows that there is only one more thing he needs to complete his sense of exultation, and that is someone with whom he can share the joys of the street. Thus, the song's final affirmation, repeated over and over as though in chant, is a call to his girl—indeed, to all his comrades and kindred spirits—to "meet me out in the street." There in that place of total honesty and spontaneity, he knows that his joy and aliveness will only be magnified by sharing them with others.

Or Is It Something Worse?

Could it be that with *The River,* Bruce Springsteen finally has come to understand that the uncommitted life is not worth living? The question of marriage concerns the heart of *The River,* the last two songs with which he concludes the album's first record. But these two songs—"I Wanna Marry You" and the album's title track— certainly offer markedly differing visions of matrimony.

In "I Wanna Marry You" the singer is proposing to a single mother with two children, one of them still in a baby carriage. Her life is difficult, perhaps even bleak. She never smiles or even speaks. "Must be a lonely life for a working girl," the singer commiserates, and he offers her his hand in marriage.

It is not that he sees himself as a sort of condescending savior, out to rescue her single-handedly from her depressing fate, or to dominate her and keep her barefoot and pregnant forever. "Now honey, I don't want to clip your wings," he tells her.

Nor has he been besotted with the idea of romance. Just before his death, his father had warned him that "true, true love is just a lie." But his father "went to his grave a broken heart," the singer laments. He died a victim of his own cynicism, unable to find fulfillment in giving his heart to another. It is a tragedy the son seems determined not to repeat.

"In the end," he agrees, "true love can't be some fairy tale." True love, he seems to be saying—the love he acknowledges that he wears "without shame"—points toward something more complex. What he offers the young woman is a union founded on mutual caring and a deep sense of responsibility.

"Life has taught us that love does not consist in gazing at each other but in looking outward in the same direction," the noted French author Antoine de Saint-Exupery once wrote. It is that kind of solid, durable, love-for-the-long-haul that the narrator in "I Wanna Marry You" seems intent on fostering. The tragedy is that all the good intentions in the world cannot protect the most decent of men and women against the vicissitudes of life in this world, which is so often a veil of tears.

Barely has the hopeful and edifying proposal of "I Wanna Marry You" been issued than it is dashed against the rocks in Springsteen's hauntingly beautiful song "The River." This is an epic song, whose narrative is based on the experience of Springsteen's sister, Pamela, and her family. Springsteen watched as they struggled to survive financially after his brother-in-law—just like the main character in the song—lost a good-paying construction job. "That's my life," Pamela exclaimed to her brother backstage, after hearing him sing "The River" for the first time.[7]

The song's power and poignancy seem firmly rooted in the trials and heartaches of palpably real women and men. Almost from the start, one perceives the stifling boundaries and low expectations. We are told that down in the valley—down in the unremarkable, gray, industrial wasteland that it represents—you're brought up to live the same life your parents did, "to do like your daddy done." Nothing else is to be expected from life; higher aspirations will only end in disappointment.

But the glory of youth is that it aspires anyway. Youth rebels, and pushes back boundaries, and seeks those idyllic places "where the fields [are] green."

Youth also fades, of course, and eventually withers. Or it comes crashing to a halt when something like an out-of-wedlock pregnancy comes to pass. Then there will be no long, drawn-out adolescence extending into the middle-to-late-twenties. There will be "a union card and a wedding coat" for the father-to-be, and a perfunctory, shotgun ceremony at the courthouse for the mother. There the judge will "put it all to rest" in a procedure sounding more like a funeral than a wedding, with no smiles for the camera, no flowers, no fancy wedding dress.

But the energy of youth still hangs on, as do the late-night rides back to the river that now symbolizes those stolen younger days. There is even the flash of hope as a decent job is secured.

But the hope is just a flicker; it is barely announced when it's gone, and the layoff slip arrives. And the baby is born. And any pretense of an easy life evaporates, "vanished right into the air."

Soon the young husband and wife—so old beyond their years now—realize that they are better off not dreaming or hoping at all, because then they no longer run the risk of seeing everything they desire mocked in this seemingly cursed life they lead. The river of life has overwhelmed and exhausted them. The husband has retreated into denial and can't remember what he once hoped for; the wife now is subsumed by apathy and doesn't care. What memories they still have taunt them; their lives grow colder still in remembrance of those times when they still felt alive: she with her body "tan and wet down at the reservoir" and he, in his virile youth, protective and passionate. "Is a dream a lie if it don't come true?" Springsteen finally explodes in the classic line. "Or is it something worse?"

They may have precious little to show for their exhaustion. Their river has run dry, and they lie bitter and broken beside its banks. But if those memories still have the power to haunt them, then perhaps they are, at least, still alive. Perhaps something of that old passion still stirs within them, if it can still hold power over them. The river of life—in all of its fluidity and transitoriness and change—still offers their best hope of transformation. They will never pretend again that it can be easy. The small hope that it may at least be possible must be enough.

Caught You in Their Sights

But don't look for things to get better anytime soon. Few songs in the Springsteen canon capture the sense of disappointed hopes more hauntingly than "Point Blank," with which *The River*'s second record begins.

There is an inexorable decline that is carved at the heart of life, the narrator in "Point Blank" points outs. Naively, we might hope that everything will be all right tomorrow. But it probably won't: "tomorrows fall in number, in number one by one." Certainly, life goes on: the sun will come up, and we will awaken to a new day. But with each new day, we're dying; with each tomorrow, we move perceptibly closer to our own demise.

Life—its betrayals, its disappointments, its deferred hopes— wounds us, sometimes fatally. Sometimes it shoots us in the back with its surreptitious, incessant claims and its demands, slights, and slurs. Sometimes it shoots us right between the eyes with a full frontal attack on our sensibilities, dignity, hopes and dreams. The "pretty lies" to which we were clinging—the tenuous hopes and aspirations we might have had—ultimately are exposed as merely more shattered promises, lying like so much debris along the roadside.

Life is hard, and we "grow up fast." We take what we're given and do what we're told, even when the demands we face are hurtful to body, soul, and self. Eventually we learn that there is slim hope of any redemption issuing forth from human hands, and that there are lots of things we want that we'll never have, and lots of promises that don't get kept. As in Shakespeare, the Romeos that enter our lives can't quite pull it off. Then when all the "little white lies" we tell ourselves "to ease the pain" (and mitigate the starkness and bleakness of life) are blown away, finally "the lights go out"; our illusions are shattered, and we are brought face to face with the emptiness of it all.

Oftentimes the sweeter and more blessed the memories we have, the more disappointing and bitter the realization that without hope, we are, each one of us, "just another stranger waitin' to get blown away." When love leaves, we each become just another forlorn sojourner waiting for death. Only remembering how to love kindles within us the will—the "fight" we need—to save ourselves from self-annihilation.

As stated earlier, when he was in the process of finalizing his selections for *The River*, Springsteen worried how some of his more downbeat and pensive ballads could coexist on the same record with buoyant, full-band rockers. But all of us, at various points in our lives, spend a good deal of time balanced on the cusp between darkness and light: wanting to throw in the towel one day; luxuriating in the warmth of love and the laughter of friends the next. So it is on the second record of *The River* that the forces of hope and despair seem to alternate with each other, song by song (and oftentimes within the same song). "Point Blank" is the album's emotional nadir. From this point, we have at least the consolation that things have got to get better.

The despair of "Point Blank" is followed by the energy and exuberance of "Cadillac Ranch." But in spite of the song's upbeat tempo, the subject of the song is once again the fear of death and abandonment. The original Cadillac Ranch is a large public work of art near Amarillo, Texas—a series of ten Cadillacs, buried nose-down in the ground at the edge of a wheat field.

Springsteen grasped the Cadillac Ranch as a vivid metaphor for the transitoriness of all existence, of how that which was once powerful, and elite, and so very much desired becomes, with the passage of time, obsolete, exhausted, and fully expendable. It isn't that the ending is so fearsome or terrifying; Springsteen acknowledges that death comes to all that is, and that such is, after all, simply the natural order of things. He knows that someday he, too, will join his pa, and his aunt, and all the generations that have come before him—even James Dean, and Burt Reynolds, and NASCAR driver Junior Johnson, to name the few he names—down at the Cadillac Ranch, that is, among the ranks of those who have gone before.

It's not the fact that he has to go—eventually—that irks Springsteen. He just doesn't want it to be anytime soon. He wants to live before he dies. He doesn't want to be old before his time, or discarded while there is still life in him. He doesn't want to be carted off and buried while he is still breathing.

"I'm a rocker," Springsteen sings defiantly in the next song. He tells his girl that his James Bond watch and *I Spy* beeper and his Batmobile all still work—as do the more embodied tools of his trade, we might imagine. He has what it takes to rescue a girl in distress, and to keep her satisfied.

"I'm a rocker," he sings, as though trying to convince himself, as much as his baby, perhaps. Maybe this rocker protests his endurance and stamina a bit too much and a bit too aggressively (as does his cohort in the even more explicit "Ramrod"). But there is something inspiring, nonetheless, in a fulsome spirit that refuses to be trammeled. Springsteen here is singing praises once again that even in less-than-ideal times and circumstances, the cup of life has a way of overflowing.

Fading Away

At other times, the light burning in the soul grows dim. It comes perilously close to being snuffed out.

A man's lover finds a more understanding partner, and a relationship comes to an end. "I don't wanna fade away," Springsteen sings, as though in the death of their relationship he glimpses the death of his own soul. The years have taken something from them; indeed, they have killed whatever it was about their relationship that made it real in the first place. Now there is just a sense of longing as they look back at what they once had, in those "days when you and I walked as two." There are now just great empty spaces (and a growing sense of darkness and gloom) where there were once large rooms filled with light and joy and music and dancing.

They both seem to be resigned to the fact that their relationship is dead. She, at least, has found the strength to move on and to build a new life, albeit with someone else. He seems to have ceded the field to his new rival; he will not just hang around and be a "useless memory," a ghost from the past. He doesn't want simply to "vanish into the night," though without the one he once loved to light his way, he seems to have no idea of what he can now do to avoid his soul's fading away.

Even more threatened by self-annihilation is the narrator of the next song, "Stolen Car." So total is this man's psychic desolation that he has traded a sense of real selfhood for the cheap ecstasy of being caught stealing cars. But even at this he's a failure. Each night he waits to get caught, but he never does.

Why has this man sunk so low? Things had started out looking pretty good: "I met a little girl and I settled down," he sings; they even had a house in a nice part of town. But the house, and the job, and the material possessions just weren't enough.

Perhaps the experience of this man and his wife indicates the kind of assault our sense of selfhood faces in this competitive, frenetic, accumulative culture of ours. This man's experience may be extreme, but it's hardly atypical. It is not hard to spot the alienation on the faces of so many people around us as they engage in their daily activities: caught in traffic along one of the highways ringing a major American city; waiting at the station for their train into town; dropping the kids off at school in the morning; hurrying up to buy groceries for supper. So many of Springsteen's characters seem mired in economic deprivation; they subsist at the lower economic strata of society, far removed from a comfortable middle class American lifestyle. But the character in "Stolen Car" reminds us that it takes more than a nice little house and a comfortable lifestyle to keep the fires of the soul burning and our relationships alive.

Ties (Still) Binding

As *The River* flows steadily toward its endpoint, Springsteen manages one more bit of anthemic glory. In "The Price You Pay" there are echoes of the defiant hopefulness of earlier works. It is not difficult to discern echoes here from "The Promised Land," including a final verse where all reminders of failure are taken up and cast aside.

Up to this point, any sense of hopefulness we have felt in *The River* has certainly been more equivocal and oblique. *The River* is, after all, not an album about transcendence but about sheer survival. The characters here aren't capable of great shows of bravado celebrating their ultimate victories over the powers that be. They would, all of them, be satisfied with gaining a draw in the great battle of life and making it through another day without a major catastrophe befalling them or those they love. "The Price You Pay," with its heroic allusions to "hands held high" reaching out "for the open skies" and Moses resting at the edge of the "chosen land" is certainly atypical of the album as a whole.

But Bruce Springsteen nevertheless demonstrates here that a youthful heart, rich with deep ideals, still beats within him. In spite of all that he has witnessed and experienced, there is still plenty of warmth in the blood that flows in his veins. He may sing songs weighted with the downbeat experience of real people. But such songs of real experience still resonate on occasion with the spirit of creative innocence that blessed him from the first.

But while "The Price You Pay" honors the experience (and recounts some of the travails) of these dear, hard souls we have met down by this riverside, it is not the fitting song with which to end this journey. Its hope is genuine but nonetheless still too idealized. *The River* is an album of loose edges and unresolved contradictions. We need to feel the river's grit in our hands at least one more time before we move on.

As with Springsteen in general (and certainly with this album in particular), the ending can't come too quickly. As in attending a Springsteen concert, we have to know we've been through something major—and that we've invested a significant amount of time in the struggle. So it is that we are charged to endure the almost eight-and-one-half minutes of the album's penultimate song, the overwrought "Drive All Night."

This is not to say that the song isn't a fount of genuine, deep emotion. The singer here may be relatively poor in material possessions, but he lacks nothing in soul. His feelings are genuine and his dedication complete, which is why when the breakup with his mate comes it is so devastating: "When I lost you, honey, sometimes I think I lost my guts, too," he begins. Losing her has ripped the insides out of him. All that could be taken—everything he ever prized, and loved, and wanted to hold tight in his arms—has been taken from him. The ties that bound her to him have been severed, and he now is hemorrhaging emotionally—a hemorrhage that just won't stop.

Neither will the song. It goes on and on as the man professes his love and loyalty, and as he thinks back over the days of his life and tries to conjure up what he could have done differently in order to hold on to the woman he loved. He would sacrifice his entire life to her most basic needs and desires; he would drive all night— through any kind of inclement weather—"just to buy [her] some shoes" if that would bring her back.

He knows that defeat beckons: the fallen angels and the calling, crying strangers have his number; they will be coming for him soon. Only a reunion with the woman of his dreams will save him now, a reunion that will never come.

Finally, in *The River*'s last song, Springsteen reduces the precious human equation to its most basic elements. One man stares mortality straight in the face and once more implicitly declares, as did the singer way back on the album's first song, "Blest be the ties that bind."

The images put forth in "Wreck on the Highway" are vivid, even cinematic: A man is driving down a dark highway "at the end of the working day" when he comes across an accident scene. A stranger lies dying by the side of the road and implores the singer to help him. An ambulance arrives and takes the man to the hospital, but we can infer that it's too late and that the man will die from his injuries.

As the song's narrator watches the ambulance pull away, his thoughts are not with the accident victim any longer but with those who will survive him. He is no longer dwelling on the past ("What happened?") or even on the present ("How bad is he hurt?"), but rather his eyes are fixed on the future, in the consequences of this dark and tragic night. He thinks of the people who love this man and how their lives will be changed, changed utterly, by what has happened along this highway. In a profound moment of compassion, he senses his connection—with this man he does not know; with the man's family and loved ones, whom he has never met; indeed, with all of those with whom he shares the certainty of death and the power of love.

That brings the preciousness and fragility of life home to him—literally. When he gets back to his house, he gazes at the woman he loves, now deep in sleep. He holds her close and clings to her for dear life, physically reinforcing the ties that connect each of them to one another.

James Baldwin once wrote, "The sea rises, the light fails, lovers cling to each other, and children cling to us. The moment we cease to hold each other, the moment we break faith with one another, the sea engulfs us and the light goes out."[8]

These lives we lead often fray the ties that bind. So many forces—economic, social, cultural, interpersonal—buffet the connections we have with one another. The currents of life can often threaten our little crafts.

Yet there is something in the river's flow that lifts us free. We are headed, through all the shoals of life, toward that Great Sea where all rivers end. Our power may seem limited and fragile, but there is something in us that shares the greater powers of all creation. If we keep faith with Life—and that means keeping faith with each other—then when our journeys finally end, we too may be bruised and battered, but we will find ourselves at last on a vast but friendly shore.

Chapter Six

Facing Sin and Evil
Nebraska

Springsteen followed the commercial success of *The River* with a most unusual album that was composed of a series of songs he had recorded on a four-track Teac tape machine set up in the bedroom of his home in Colts Neck, New Jersey.

Springsteen had returned home to New Jersey in late 1981 physically and emotionally exhausted. He had spent almost two years in the studio recording *The River* and had followed the album's release with a long and arduous road tour. Two years was too long to record an album, he thought. He needed to find a faster way of bringing his songs to life, a more genuine and spontaneous milieu in which to create. Springsteen later described it this way: "I told Mike [Batlan], the guy that does my guitars, 'Mike, go get a tape player so I can record these songs.' I figured what takes me so long in the studio is not having the songs written. So I said I'm gonna write 'em, and I'm gonna tape 'em. If I can make them sound good enough with just me, then I know they'll be fine. Then I can play 'em with the band."[1] Batlan set up the cassette recorder in the bedroom of the house Springsteen was renting in Colts Neck. Then, on January 3, 1982, in Christopher Sandford's words, "Springsteen settled onto a bedroom chair, turned on a four-track cassette deck and picked up his guitar."[2] Within three hours, according to Sandford, Springsteen had recorded his sixth album, as well as a good half dozen additional songs.

Eventually, Springsteen and the E Street Band went into the

studio to turn the tape that had been recorded that day into an album fit for commercial release. A variety of mixes and arrangements were attempted; various embellishments and accompaniments were added, then subtracted. But nothing seemed to work. The songs seemed to sound better with just Springsteen's voice— raw, unadorned, accompanied only by acoustic guitar and an occasional bit of harmonica—than they did in full-band arrangements. Eventually, Springsteen and his manager, Jon Landau, decided to release most of the songs on the original demo as they were— "bare," as Springsteen described them.[3] Reluctantly, the bigwigs at Columbia, reassured by Landau's promise that Springsteen's next album would be a "real rocker," agreed. *Nebraska* was released in September 1982.

"On *Nebraska*," Springsteen was "almost singing to himself," Landau said later, "unusually softly," as though he were singing from some dark and frightened place within.[4] He seemed a man alone in all the world, pondering the depths of existence and not liking what he saw there. Staring off into the void of meaninglessness and despondency, Springsteen crafted a series of songs about people completely isolated from all those forces that keep men and women sane and give their lives meaning. *Nebraska*, Springsteen said, was about "what happens to people when they're alienated from their friends and their community and their government and their job."[5] When these basic touchstones of life slip away, Springsteen said, the essential constraints of society become meaningless and impotent. Then "anything can happen," and the field becomes wide open to forces of mayhem and evil.

An Evil in This World

The album's title cut tells the horrific story of Charles Starkweather, who along with his female accomplice Caril Fugate murdered eleven people in a killing spree across the American heartland in 1958. There may be very few purely evil characters in the songs of Bruce Springsteen, but Starkweather is certainly one. Unlike most of the other men and women we meet in *Nebraska*, who, whatever their failings and whatever their crimes, are usually more sinned against than sinning, Starkweather is a genuinely malevolent creature, who kills for (as he says) the "fun" of it.

The song begins on a front lawn of a home in the very center of the country—Lincoln, Nebraska, an unremarkable sort of place, where we might imagine things out of the ordinary seldom take place. A girl is practicing an all-American ritual of banality—twirling a baton—but then she gets into a car for a ride with this loner, and before the end of the first verse, ten people are dead.[6]

Springsteen's Starkweather expresses no remorse for what he's done. Rather, he seems proud of his blood-soaked accomplishments. In perhaps the song's most chilling line, he declares that, at least for a short time, he and Fugate "had us some fun." Even as he looks toward his trial and sentencing, and his inevitable execution in the electric chair, his only request is that his "pretty baby" be sitting on his lap when it happens. Even in death, theirs will be an amoral, soulless, skin-deep relationship. In their quest for "fun"—for a life not limited by any responsibility and loyalty to anything beyond their bodies' passions in a given moment— they have hurtled beyond the boundaries of civilized society. They have cut themselves off from any source of abiding comfort and peace.

Where lies the source of this evil? Not in any malevolent supernatural power that has won this vile pair over to the power of its ways. Nor does it lie in any ultimate taint upon our nature as human beings. "There's just a meanness in this world," Springsteen's Starkweather declares, and he has chosen to let it be his master. Ultimately, Starkweather chose the complete heartlessness of a life that exploded in malice against all social connections and deeper relationships. His was the utter callousness that results when a person turns his back on all those forces that hold life together and provide it with some vestige of meaning.

So Starkweather and Fugate stand condemned—in human eyes, through the justice system—but further, they stand condemned in the consciousness of eternity as well. Without connection to anything enduring or substantial—to no ideals, no purpose, no greater love—Starkweather's soul is now destined to "be hurled" into "that great void" where it will wander endlessly, ultimately alienated from any and all hope of salvation.

Others, of course, take a more tortuous route down the road toward wrongdoing. When the auto plant in Mahwah, New Jersey, is closed down, a worker named Ralph reaches the end of his rope. He goes out, gets drunk, and gets a gun. By the end of the first verse of the song "Johnny 99," a night clerk has been shot.

However, there will be no Starkweather-like killing spree here: in the second verse, Ralph is captured and thrown into a police cruiser. By the end of the third, he has been sentenced to ninety-nine years in prison. "The evidence is clear," the judge intones, and along with the sentence he slaps on Ralph a nickname—"Johnny 99."

Unlike Starkweather, Ralph has other connections to the world: people who are not as sure as the judge that this sentence does, indeed, "fit the crime." As soon as the sentence is handed down, Ralph's family raises a ruckus in the courtroom. His girlfriend has to be taken away. His mother, too, raises her voice in support of her son. His family, at least, insists that "Johnny 99" get his hearing, a real day in court. And so, Ralph makes his statement: "I got debts no honest man could pay," he protests to the judge. He had lost his job, and was about to lose his house—his family's home—and that had rendered him desperate. This doesn't excuse his actions, Ralph agrees; it doesn't mean he's innocent. But it does explain how a one-time rational being could lose control over his thoughts, how his view of the world could become skewed toward the criminal, and how he could ultimately come to see his life as no longer worth living.

Lines of responsibility are not always cut and dried, Johnny wants the judge to know. Sometimes, evil results when a society turns its back on its people. When people are treated as mere cogs in a machine, or numbers in a ledger—mere human "resources" rendered expendable in defense of the almighty "bottom line"— then it is the society that bears the first wave of the blame for the mayhem that well might ensue. When men and women feel as though society has declared them worthless and redundant, they may well take depraved and despicable actions in response.

Luck May Have Died

Sometimes the very living of life takes its toll. People grow old and tired; energy wanes. Throughout this long trudge through life, we die a little more each day—in every slight, every abusive relationship, every disappointment, every time we have been misunderstood or undervalued or taken for granted. Life takes a toll on many levels.

Sometimes the toll is corporate: entire communities lie passed by and outmoded, with their best years long behind them; they hang on as mere shadows of what they once were. In the case of Atlantic City, New Jersey, they cast a malevolent shadow, in the midst of which huddles poverty and crime. As the song "Atlantic City" begins, the forces of evil seem on the verge of taking over: the Mob is on a rampage, blowing up the homes of all who stand in their way; the once fashionable boardwalk now seems the dwelling place of corruption's final victory. Counterforces of law and order seem harried and ineffectual.

The city has ended up at the bottom of the socioeconomic pecking order, and so have its people. They have "caught on the wrong side of that line" that separates winners and losers. Whatever grandiose dreams he may have—dreams of sandcastles of changed luck rising along the boardwalk like so many new casinos—the narrator of "Atlantic City" also has "debts that no honest man can pay." His only choice, then, would seem to be to let his debts crush him—or to sell himself to the service of the forces of dishonesty and malice that now seem ascendant. There would seem to be no happy or honest option open to him at this point.

He may hope—he may even think he believes—that he and his mate are really headed out to "where the sand's turnin' to gold." He may think that he can do what he needs to do to sustain their bodies, without losing his soul. But barely does he utter this absurd hope to his partner when the bleak reality of their situation assaults him straight in the face: "Put on your stockin's baby," he tells her in the very same breath, "'cause the night's getting cold." Illogical fantasies of some oceanside paradise offer little comfort to people who are probably living on the street.

It is clear here that the world is going to hell, and that the center is no longer holding. The ordinary men and women who bear life's burden are destined to receive no more relief than the overwhelmed district attorney. Like the hapless gambling commission, they too are hanging on by the skin of their teeth.

The present assaults us with its cruelty. The future assaults us with its menace. Even the past won't leave us alone; it threatens to return to haunt us as well. "Maybe everything that dies someday comes back," the song tells us. But not everything that dies *should* come back. Not all risings from the dead are fortuitous; it is more often malevolent ghosts who return from the dead than it is glorified saviors. The world, no doubt, would be better off if the majority of specters from the past crawled back into their graves and stayed dead.

Springsteen intimates here that much of the accumulated psychological or interpersonal baggage that drives people to desperation arises out of no fault of their own. Such "debts" are often accrued through fortune or accident or oppressive social structures that stack the deck against them from the start.

There is often music amid the decay, of course. Even amid the ruin, life gives off a suggestive whirr that could be taken for harmony, even power. The road may seem "Open All Night," and life may seem chock-full of possibilities. But before long we realize that the souped-up vehicle we are charging around in is all baling wire and DayGlo paint—all show and no go. In time, as the illusion of our power wanes, we may actually comprehend the truth that a fantasy of a turbojet does not a spaceship make. While the dark of night might hide the worst corruptions of the day, this "spooky" turnpike has a malevolence of its own that will, within a short enough time, give way to the desolation of "New Jersey in the mornin' like a lunar landscape"—with terrors of its own that we can only imagine.

The world pictured in "Open All Night" is quite a living hell, but there are at least some fleeting connections with those around us. The narrator of the song can at least enjoy the carnal pleasures of Wanda, the waitress from Bob's Big Boy, a relationship complete with buckets of fried chicken on the front seat and nighttime

trysts at a hallowed place romantically named "Scrap Metal Hill."
They may not be permanent and abiding pleasures, but at least they
get us (barely) through the night.

But by five in the morning the night is over, and whatever fleeting mysteries it held are now long gone. "Oil pressure's sinkin'
fast," we are told, and all that beckons now is the living death that
daylight brings. There are no more haunted specters now, just
another red ball sun rising over the towers of the refinery. The pain
and terror of the world are now out in the open. Even the music has
grown perverted: it's all gospel stations now—heavy-handed religion that circumvents the mystery and kills the spirit. The real high
priest of the night, Mr. Deejay, seems nowhere to be found. The
singer's last prayer for transcendence will go unanswered. There
will be no rock and roll savior this time to deliver him from this
nowhere life he has been destined to lead.

In "State Trooper," a twin song to "Drive All Night," the surroundings are similar, but the decline into the abyss is even more
precipitous. This driver, too, is cruising down the New Jersey Turnpike late at night. Relay towers and oil refineries once again dot the
landscape. The radio again fails to offer any salvation: this time it
is talk shows that jam the airwaves, their incessant chatter squeez-
ing out all the poetry and holy mystery of life.

This driver, too, prays for deliverance "from nowhere." But
unlike the narrator of "Drive All Night," who was at least hurrying
home *toward* something—another tryst with Wanda on Scrap
Metal Hill perhaps—the drive in "State Trooper" is all about
escape, about getting *away* from something. This driver is fleeing
some deep inner pain—an inner hurt or scar, a crime he has committed, some past abuse—which he has carried around with him
"his whole life." Now he wants to run as far as possible from the
meaningless, desolate life he has led up till now.

But he knows, too, the forces that stand in his way: all those
insensitive, passionless, unimaginative vestiges of authority more
powerful than he, exemplified in the person of the state trooper to
whom the song is addressed. The driver knows that if he can avoid
these powers that be, even for a little while—and carve out some
small space of personal autonomy and identity for himself—then

he might at least hope for some semblance of release. But his "last prayer"—"Hi ho silver-o deliver me from nowhere"—seems delivered into a night that is all emptiness and void. At this low point there is probably no one left out there to listen, no vestige of connection tying him to a life that might actually have meaning.

Nothin' Feels Better Than Blood on Blood

When hope comes for the characters in *Nebraska*, it arrives through the caring, warmth, and compassion of members of their families. But there is no place in the austere vision of this album for a tender or romanticized perspective even here. The connection these characters feel with their kin may offer them a bit of hope, some small warmth, and even a trace of enjoyment in their lives. But with family, as with all human relationships, nothing is a sure bet. As human experience from the time of Cain and Abel forward has shown, there is no guarantee that the time, energy, and care we expend upon our families will ever be repaid—or will even be proven worth the trouble.

In a fallen world like that presented in *Nebraska,* it should come as no surprise that the family is often a fallen and dysfunctional institution, as well. If our families can comfort and succor us, they can wound us—deeply, even indelibly. It is in the realm of the family that we are first given the breath of life and in which we open our eyes to life's possibilities. But this deep tie of blood that binds us so closely to others can, very often, be transformed from a lifeline into a noose.

Joe Roberts, the main character and narrator of the song "Highway Patrolman," is certainly a responsible sort. His belief in integrity and civic virtue nearly leaps out of the first lines, where he tells us his name and quickly adds, "I work for the state." More specifically, Roberts is a sergeant in the highway patrol: a staunch and honest defender of the status quo.

But then Joe tells us that he has a brother named Franky, "and Franky ain't no good," he admits. The dramatic tension—in the song and in Roberts's life—is clearly established.

Throughout their lives together, Joe tells us, he's been bailing Franky out of trouble. If it was some other common hood doing the things Franky has done, there's no doubt that Joe would have written him off long ago—there would have been no second chances. But Franky is Joe's brother, and so sometimes (many times, in fact) he has decided to "look the other way." No doubt this bothers Joe deeply; he is not one who is comfortable with bending the rules.

But Joe believes that family trumps everything. To him, there is nothing in this life that is more important than the bonds of family: "nothin' feels better than blood on blood." Indeed, someone who denigrates this bond—or ignores it, or consciously severs it— someone who "turns his back" on his family, is beneath contempt, Joe believes.

Why does Joe Roberts defend familial bonds so vehemently— and, more particularly, why does he go to such lengths to protect his errant brother, whom he himself has just declared is completely worthless? Something more than brotherly love is motivating him here, and his motives are not entirely altruistic. His emotions toward his brother are much more conflicted than that.

Joe tells the story of those earlier years between him and Franky, years before his brother went completely bad, apparently. Franky was always a raucous spirit, always in trouble, even as a kid. But he and Joe shared many good times together nonetheless. They even shared, apparently, to one degree or another, the affections of the same woman—Maria—with whom they would both dance at the local bar. Then, in 1965, their paths parted: Franky went into the army (and got shipped off to Vietnam for three years), and Joe got a draft deferment, became a farmer, and married Maria.

Both brothers faced adversity, certainly: Franky fighting in the jungles of Southeast Asia, Joe trying (with little success) to make a go of it as a farmer. In 1968, Franky came home from Vietnam; Joe gave up the farm and became a highway patrolman instead. But while both brothers faced challenges in life, is there any doubt which one was dealt the better hand? Joe has ended up with the girl, the good job, and the respect of society. All Franky has is his reputation as a troublemaker and any new ghosts that have followed him home from Vietnam. Is there any wonder that Joe feels some need—perhaps out of guilt—to protect him, even if that means bending a few of his precious rules and regulations?

The denouement comes one night when Franky just about kills someone in a barroom brawl in a roadhouse near the Michigan state line. When he hears that his brother has been involved, Joe quite literally turns his back on the mess at the roadhouse—including a victim who may be near death—and jumps in his car to pursue his brother once again. After a frantic, high-speed chase, he finally catches up with Franky's Buick. But then, just before the border, Joe pulls off to the side of the road and lets his brother escape into Canada.

Joe Roberts has kept faith with Franky even to the end of the earth. Perhaps he hopes, as he watches the taillights of his brother's car disappear, that the guilt and remorse he feels about his relationship with Franky will finally fly away across the border as well. But by putting the demands of family first and turning his back on his duty, Joe may have ceded too much in the bargain. He has, in a sense, joined his brother on the side of lawlessness. Joe has stayed true to his credo that family trumps everything. But, this time at least, this victory of family has been purchased at the price of his integrity, and perhaps at the cost of a greater defeat for society at large.

Members of a family share so much: joys and sorrows, victories and defeats, achievements and deprivations. They drink from a deep, common well of good times and bad. The Buddhist monk Thich Nhat Hahn reminds us that time can harden the pain, anger, and frustration that dwell within us, until these negative emotions crystallize into internal formations that can tie us up inside and obstruct our freedom to live out life fully.[7] The pains, slights, and insults of the past—especially perhaps those directed against the family to which we belong—can bind us with a core of shame we might well carry around with us all the days of our lives.

These offenses against our psyches that wound us so deeply can seem so small in hindsight: In the case of the autobiographical song "Used Cars," it is the inability of Springsteen's father to scrape together adequate financing to purchase a brand new car—thus relegating his wife and children to the used car ghetto seemingly forever.

The closest this family will get to a new car is the test drive down Freehold's Michigan Avenue with which the song begins. Barely back at the dealership, the deal has already fallen through: as the mother fingers her wedding band, pondering, no doubt, both the depths of emotion and the limited prospects that this union represents; as the salesman stares at the father's rough and weathered hands, recognizing the obvious disconnect between how hard someone works and how much money he earns.

Whether or not the men in the neckties decide that he is "credit worthy," the young Springsteen here knows that his father is truly worthy, on a much deeper level. He knows how hard his father works at that "same job from mornin' to morn," and how, for all his hard work, he still lives in the same rundown, working class neighborhood, is still unappreciated and ridiculed by the people among whom he lives, and is still driving around in a used car—albeit a "brand new used car" this time!

The emotion that wells up in the narrator as he witnesses all this is, not surprisingly, *anger.* But there is also some sense in Springsteen's defiant and rebellious tone—and in his underlying questioning of the ultimate injustice of this whole situation—that this anger might actually empower him to make something better of his life because of what he has been through. We believe him when he sings that he "ain't ever gonna ride in no used car again."

Of course, our knowledge of Springsteen's subsequent experience—and of how his number did, indeed, come in—big time—makes it all the easier for us to trust in his bravado. But even if Springsteen had never become one of the greatest rock stars of all time (and a wealthy man in the process), there is something in his sincerity in "Used Cars" that can touch us deeply. In wanting a better life than he had as a child, he is not merely seeking to cash in on his "share" of the economic pie. Rather, he is out to redeem his entire family: the hard work of his father, the self-sacrifice of his mother, the childlike expectation of his little sister. We can feel his yearning that these people he loves should be justified in the end. Through his yearning, we too long for that day when his little sister is back in that front seat of that brand new car, blowin' that horn just as loudly as she can.

But if the passage of time hardens us, it can also serve to present some of the deprivations and challenges of the past in a softer light. Often, people who have risen from harsh economic circumstances to a somewhat more comfortable level will look back on their lives as children and say something like, "We never knew we were poor." In an age of more modest economic expectations (and less intrusive advertising pressures) everyone seemed to be roughly at the same economic level. People made do with what they had, scaled down their expectations that they would ever have substantially more, and found more imaginative (and less costly) ways of amusing themselves.

This is not to say we all dwelled happily ever after in a completely classless society. Even in those days when "we never knew we were poor," there were other people whom we knew, quite frankly, were rich. We understood that they were different from us. Their children went to different schools. They wore business suits on the streets instead of work clothes. They lived in different parts of town. Their houses were large and often protected by high fences, or hedges, or stone walls. Just about every city or town, even of the most modest size, had its mansion on the hill.

When Springsteen sings of the "Mansion on the Hill" that he remembers from childhood, it is with neither undue nostalgia nor deep bitterness. He simply remembers that house as an abiding presence, always a backdrop to his forays around town. It served as a constant reminder of society's division into those who have little and those who have a whole lot more. The "gates of hardened steel" that completely surround the mansion served as stark reminders that there were parts of town (aspects of the American Dream perhaps) that were not open to all.

This was a reality Springsteen and those of his class simply accepted. They might pull off to the side of the road and gaze up longingly at bright lights shining forth from these hallowed halls. They might hide in the cornfields and listen to all the merriment and music going on inside. But ultimately, the social code of the day—a more rigid time before the civil rights movement, the women's movement, and the various liberation movements of the 1960s and 1970s threw open the doors on what expectations people might have for their lives—slammed shut the gate and derided as hopelessly unrealistic and naive any aspirations to become part of the crowd inside the "Mansion on the Hill."

But back home among the people of his class—those rushing home from a hard day at work—Springsteen doesn't seem to care. A deeper vision of what is truly important in life comes to him: "There's a beautiful full moon rising" directly behind the great house, shining on the good and bad, the rich and poor, alike. Those who dwell in the "Mansion on the Hill" may be able to control many things. But they do not hold ultimate control over the power of life, the sweep of the seasons, and the cycling of the days. There is a much greater force that controls these. And it is in becoming one with this force that any person's true hope shall lie.

The bonds of family can be strong and true. They provide us with our place in the world and a large part of our sense of who we are. But there is nothing absolute about them. As we have seen in "Highway Patrolman," treating them as an absolute often creates an even greater evil. So strong is the family's pull on us that perhaps the wounds which take the longest to heal are those our families have rendered unto us. Sometimes the passage of time, or the death of one of the parties involved, or the unwillingness of family members to reach out and change or compromise—or even to speak with one another—make resolution of the contradictions between various family members impossible.

In the end within a certain family, certain sins may well "lie unatoned." This is the situation at the conclusion of the haunting "My Father's House." Here again Springsteen portrays himself as a child, but this song has neither the adolescent rebelliousness of "Used Cars" nor the nostalgic patina of "Mansion on the Hill." Rather, "My Father's House" tells the story of a dream—a nightmare, really—and presents a somber portrait of a race to escape at last the clutches of ghosts from a childhood unadorned by anything but pain.

The father's house stands "shining hard and bright." In this dream, at least, it is a steadfast fortress of all that family should be: protection against the evils of the world, comfort for us in our sadness, refuge against the ordeals of life. But while the child in the song views the house from a distance, he hasn't arrived back home at his father's abode yet. Before he gets there, he has to outrun the devil ("snappin' at [his] heels"), through all the "brambles and branches" that wound and scar him.

Finally—in his dream, at least—the singer arrives back at the paternal dwelling place where the door is opened, and he falls shaking in his father's arms, safe at last. Such is the dream; such is the blessed ideal. Reality is quite different: The son awakens and decides to reconcile with his father. He goes to the house where his father once lived, stands on the porch, and knocks on the door. But the door is answered by someone he doesn't recognize—a woman, but not his mother. She is a stranger, politely sympathetic (though she doesn't invite him in; she keeps her distance and speaks to him "through a chained door," as any stranger would). When he asks for his father, the woman replies that nobody by that name lives there anymore.

The young man now knows that reconciliation isn't possible. Perhaps the father is dead. Perhaps the father and son have just grown so distant that no bridge of shared experience exists any longer to connect them. Perhaps they are just doomed to be strangers to one another now, through the remainder of their days.

The father's house still stands, the son says, "like a beacon" calling to him in his dreams. But now it shines not as a guiding light of hope and courage but as a stern sentinel reminding him of how far his path has strayed from the way of right relations.

At the End of Every Hard-Earned Day

Someone once asked Albert Einstein what the most important question of all was. "Is the world a friendly place or not?" Einstein replied.

In our experience of the world there are plenty of times we might be tempted to answer that question in the negative. The last song on *Nebraska*, "Reason to Believe," presents several such scenarios with more than a small touch of irony.

The first came out of Springsteen's own experience. One day while driving down New Jersey Highway 33, which passes through Freehold, Springsteen saw a man standing off to the side of the road, hunched over an obviously dead dog. The man seemed determined that if he poked the dog enough times with a stick, the dog would come back to life. The experience provided the vivid image Springsteen uses to start off "Reason to Believe."

"Struck me kinda funny," Springsteen sings. Even in this completely bleak situation, the man seems to cling to his hope for a happy outcome—to his reason to believe.

The next examples Springsteen cites are less pictorial, perhaps, but no less vivid: Mary Lou is in love with a guy named Johnny, and she sacrifices her life to him. She takes care of him and gives him all her money, but to no avail. One day, he just ups and leaves her. But still—years later, we might imagine—every day Mary Lou continues to walk to the end of the dirt road near her house. She hopes that maybe this will be the day Johnny will return. He never does. But Mary Lou won't let go of her hope, her reason to believe.

The next verse is a bridge: Life isn't completely bleak, of course. Even in the midst of tragedy and absurdity, there are reasons to hope and to rejoice. An old man's life draws to a close, and he passes away in a lonely shack in the woods. A new baby—Kyle William—is born and baptized, and his whole life stands before him. Of course, in time, that life too will draw to a close: baby Kyle will become the old man breathing his last. His days may well be as "hard earned" as anyone else's, as full of long labor and short sweetness. "The poor person toils to make a meager living," says the apocryphal book of Sirach (31:4). Certainly, nothing we have witnessed in any of the songs on *Nebraska* will contradict that proclamation.

Finally, in the last verse of "Reason to Believe," everyone is gathered for a wedding. The congregation is there. The preacher is there. The groom is there. Hopes are high. But the bride never arrives. Everyone leaves, except the groom. He just stands there, perhaps waiting for his love finally to appear; perhaps because he is too numb to go anywhere else. He stands there and watches the river flow on—as his life will flow on, whatever this hard day ultimately brings. He knows that as long as he is still alive, there is still hope—still a reason to believe.

There is always the possibility that this hope will be absurdly misplaced. No amount of poking and prodding will make that dog "get up and run." But even though the dog is dead, life goes on. Sooner or later, the bridegroom will be forced to leave that spot by the river which promised him such bliss. Even when our little hopes die, life goes on.

A Mexican proverb affirms, "Hope dies last." Often when all else has been taken, hope remains. The reasons we have for continuing to hope are our little encapsulations of that "deathless, faithful, coming into life again" from which, in the end, none of the absurdity or tragedy of this world can sever us.

But Einstein's question remains: "Is the world a friendly place or not?" Does the world support human hopes and aspirations? Is life, ultimately, a good thing? Science cannot answer that question, Einstein believed. Only the human spirit can. It is, the great scientist believed, a question for religion to answer, a question for us to ponder in the depths of our spirits. Life cycles on and on, over and over, and we who observe the great circle of life must simply remain humble at the mystery of it all.

Chapter Seven

American Ambiguity
Born in the U.S.A.

*L*andau had promised the executives at Columbia Records that Bruce's next album would be a real rocker. But the process of finally getting that album recorded would prove to be an arduous one. There were perhaps a half dozen full-band versions of songs that Springsteen had originally recorded acoustically during the at-home *Nebraska* sessions. These might form the core of the next album, Landau thought, but it was also necessary for Springsteen to get back in the studio with the band and record additional material.

That was something Springsteen seemed reticent to do. In the period following *Nebraska,* "his heart was elsewhere," according to Dave Marsh.[1] Instead of arranging for recording time at one of his usual venues back east, Bruce had driven across country to Los Angeles. There he even had a recording studio constructed in the garage of the house he was renting, in which he continued to experiment with the kind of solo, acoustic work he had found so satisfying on *Nebraska.* Executives at Columbia were increasingly concerned that Springsteen now was on one coast, while his manager—and his band—were on the other, more than three thousand miles away. They were afraid, Springsteen said, "about me making another record in my garage or in my bedroom or wherever I was makin' it."[2] Finally, in May 1983, at Landau's insistence, Springsteen flew back east, and he and the band settled into the Hit Factory in New York to continue recording his seventh album.

Back to Vietnam

There was one song on the *Nebraska* demo that Landau, among others, hadn't thought much of. It was a song about a Vietnam veteran, sung solo by Springsteen and accompanied by a defiant and haunting series of guitar chords, with a bit of Bruce's screeching and moaning dubbed in as background afterward. It "didn't even seem like a particularly good song," Landau said later.[3] It had something of an "alien" quality about it, he said, and didn't quite come up to the quality of the songs that were eventually released on *Nebraska.*

Due to injuries received in a motorcycle accident in 1968 (as well as a convincing job feigning insanity during his pre-induction interview), Springsteen himself had narrowly escaped being drafted and shipped off to fight in Vietnam. But his opposition to the war had never faltered, nor had his concern for those who had been forced to go to war. He was also deeply moved by the book *Born on the Fourth of July,* the autobiography of the paraplegic veteran Ron Kovic, who returned from Vietnam to become a leader of the antiwar movement. Springsteen wanted to do more to help those who had faced such horrendous conditions overseas only to return to severely diminished prospects at home.

Eventually he made contact with Bob Muller, a paraplegic ex-Marine and head of the Vietnam Veterans of America (VVA). Springsteen agreed that his show in Los Angeles in August 1981 would be done as a benefit for Muller's organization. "[Tonight] is the first step in ending the silence that has surrounded Vietnam," Springsteen declared as the concert began.[4] It was time, he said, for a concerted effort in support of the families of the 55,000 Americans who had died in Vietnam and of those who had returned from there, many of them maimed in body, mind, and spirit. The show raised nearly a quarter-million dollars and, according to Muller, saved the VVA from disbanding. "Without Bruce Springsteen, there would be no Vietnam veterans movement," Muller later declared.[5]

Back at Colts Neck later that year, Springsteen struggled to pour his feelings about Vietnam and its veterans into a song. His first

effort, which he simply titled "Vietnam," had not been entirely successful. But the song did contain within it ideas that would abide:
most strikingly the story of a Vietnam veteran who returns home
but can't find a job. The people he returns to at home profess sym-
pathy for his plight but do nothing to help him; his girlfriend has
even run off with a singer in a rock and roll band. The narrator
finally surveys the wreckage of his life and concludes that, even
though he has returned from the jungles of Asia, his life is effec-
tively over. "Now don't you understand," he asks himself, "you
died in Vietnam?"

The song "Vietnam" was put aside, but Springsteen's passion to
do something to help the veterans persisted. He revised the song's
lyrics, honing them down to their basic ideas. The result was a
much more direct and focused work, which he titled "Born in the
U.S.A."

"Born in the U.S.A." could be narrated by the same veteran as
in the earlier song, but now he speaks more forcefully and defiantly
about his plight. There is no more whining over lost girlfriends and
broken hearts. Rather, this veteran comes not so much to bemoan
his own self-abasement as to hurl fire bolts of judgment against a
society that doesn't keep faith with those who serve it. America's
treatment of its veterans had been more than shabby, Springsteen
believed. It had been a major betrayal of the social contract carved
at the heart of the American ideal. It was, further, just one more
manifestation of a society (and economic system) that increasingly
seemed to treat people as expendable, that called upon them to do
its dirty work and pursue its morally questionable policies but that
simply discarded them, or ignored them, when they no longer
served its purposes.

According to rock critic Geoffrey Himes, Springsteen believed
that "there was something wrong with a society which made a full
life so difficult to achieve." According to Himes, to Springsteen
"the Vietnam veterans were the most dramatic example of everyone who had been let down by the American dream and the rock
'n' roll promise."[6]

From the song's opening lyrics, it is obvious that the protagonist of "Born in the U.S.A." has had the deck stacked against him

from the very start: He has not been born in some bucolic American suburb or typical American locale but "in a dead man's town," and his life has been on a downward spiral since the day he was born. So abusive has life been toward him that he compares himself to a frightened dog, cowering in fear from being beaten repeatedly. But still "I was born in the U.S.A.," the singer shouts over and over again at the top of his voice. Even after everything, he still seems proud to identify himself as an *American,* with all the hope and glory that it is supposed to represent.

It is no surprise that this abused young man soon finds himself on the wrong side of the law and of society's good graces. He commits some petty crime, so to avoid prison he joins the army and is sent off as a tool of American foreign policy. When his tour of duty ends, the soldier comes home—not to a hero's welcome but to no respect and no prospects whatsoever. He can't find a job at the local refinery; even the Veterans' Administration official (who is supposed to be his advocate, after all) just brushes him off. This war has cost this returned vet dearly. He is still haunted by his memories of fighting in the jungles of Asia, and the images of his dead comrade at Khe Sahn and the woman his friend loved have carved places in his mind. Now, ten years after the war has ended, and in spite of the sacrifices he has made for his country, this veteran has absolutely nothing to show for it. He still lives his life "in the shadow of the penitentiary." Life keeps drawing him down its road, but he knows now that it is leading him nowhere.

But he was "born in the U.S.A.," he reminds us again as the song nears its conclusion. He sings the words of the chorus both defiantly and mournfully, both as a statement of pride for all this country has produced, for all of its dynamism and abundance, and as a statement of shame and rebuke from one of those denied any stake whatsoever in all that creativity and wealth.

There was no mistaking the haunted and pessimistic tone of the original acoustic version of "Born in the U.S.A." Springsteen had recorded solo as part of the *Nebraska* sessions at Colts Neck. It didn't make the cut for inclusion on *Nebraska,* but in May 1982, Springsteen tried recording a more up-tempo and full-sound version with the entire band. One night after supper, he played the notes that would become the song's evocative riff on the synthesizer for keyboardist Roy Bittan. He told the drummer, Max Weinberg, to "keep the drums going" even when the singing and the rest of the accompaniment ended, and he gave brief instructions to the other band members as to their parts. Then, as Springsteen remembered it, "We just kinda did it off the cuff. . . . There was no arrangement."[7] By the second take, the band had recorded the song that would become the title track of Springsteen's seventh album—by far the best-selling album of his entire career.

The full-band arrangement—"turbulent" and "evocative," as Jon Landau called it,[8] but also grandiose and brash and perhaps even histrionic—also helped to make "Born in the U.S.A." perhaps the most thoroughly misunderstood song in the history of rock and roll.

Late in August 1984, a couple of months into the *Born in the U.S.A.* tour, Springsteen appeared for four nights at the Capital Center, outside of Washington, D.C. In the audience for one of the shows was conservative columnist and pundit George Will, who had become intrigued by reports of the flag waving and other patriotic overtones that were said to accompany Springsteen's recent concerts. After attending about half of one of the Capital Center shows, Will filed a column entitled "A Yankee Doodle Springsteen," which appeared in newspapers across the country. In his column Will spoke of how "flags get waved" at Springsteen's concerts and of how "the recitation of closed factories and other problems always seem punctuated by a grand, cheerful affirmation: 'Born in the U.S.A.!' "[9] Will implied that "all-American" and "patriotic" values like those modeled by Springsteen were just what the country needed to keep forging ahead.

A few days later, during a stop on his reelection campaign in Hammonton, New Jersey, President Ronald Reagan attempted to cash in on Springsteen's enormous popularity in his home state. "America's future rests in a thousand dreams inside your hearts," Reagan told those who had gathered to hear him. "It rests in the message of hope in songs of a man so many young Americans admire: New Jersey's own Bruce Springsteen. And helping you make those dreams come true is what this job of mine is all about."[10]

Springsteen was livid. To see his work co-opted by the Reaganites—archconservative, probusiness Republicans who were, he felt, perhaps most culpable for many of the problems people like those in his songs faced—aggrieved him severely. On September 22, at a concert in Pittsburgh, he introduced the stark and bitter "Johnny 99" by suggesting, "I don't think [Reagan's] been listening to this one."[11] Springsteen added that he doubted whether *Nebraska* was one of the president's favorite albums.

Certainly there had been much on *Nebraska* that might have made Reagan and Will, and their Republican cohorts, squirm. But there was much on the rest of the *Born in the U.S.A.* album, too, with which they would not have been terribly comfortable either.

Just Getting Tougher

The title of "Downbound Train" alone should have warned Will, Reagan, and others that Springsteen had not been won over by their "morning in America" ideology. "Hope deferred makes the heart sick," Proverbs 13:12 states plainly. Often, as the toll of deferred hopes pile up—for some people, decades of them; for some families, generations of them—people can come to feel as though they too are riders on a "Downbound Train." Perhaps there had been a point where it felt as though things were finally coming together for us. Perhaps we had a good job and found ourselves in a good and sustaining relationship for a time. But in uncertain times—and especially in a Reaganesque culture of dog eat dog and every man for himself—this good fortune can quickly dissipate, and once-high hopes can come quickly to seem like mere illusions. Suddenly, Dame Fortune no longer smiles upon us; our luck changes; we get laid off; our mate leaves; we find ourselves caught in a dead-end job, alone, back at the bottom of the heap. All the while, we hear "that long whistle whine," and we know the train of life is still moving; the years are going by, but we (like the Vietnam vet in "Born in the U.S.A") aren't getting anywhere. Instead, we come home to a house whose emptiness mocks us. We perform the backbreaking work of laying ties for the railroad, but the engine of opportunity seems to have passed us by. "What's the use, then?" we might well ask; more likely than not, we sink into despair. "All streams run to the sea, but the sea is not full," Ecclesiastes tells us (1:7). The narrator of "Downbound Train" would surely agree that "all things are wearisome, more than one can express" (1:8). Such weariness hardly qualifies as a paean to the glories of supply-side economics.

Even the more upbeat "Cover Me"—a song as close to disco as anything Springsteen ever recorded—can also be read as a meditation on America in the Reagan era. "The times are tough now, just getting tougher," the song begins. There is no homage here, however fleeting, to the Reagan myth of a new day dawning in America. For most people, it seems, things are getting steadily worse; the roughness and coarseness of the world are on the rise. The only hope the singer has is to find a lover who will "cover" him, in whose presence (and in whose body) he can hide, and lose himself, and avoid the challenges of life.

Outside there is rain and driving snow. Against these forces of nature—and the social forces they represent—the singer wants only to retreat into a purely private life. "I ain't going out there no more," he sings. He no longer wants to face the struggles and trials life continually deals forth. "Let our love blind us," the singer implores his companion. Let us be blind to the problems of the world and lose ourselves in one another.

But such a love, founded entirely on escape from the world, is a truncated love. In its most profound sense, perhaps, love is the opposite of escape. It is by engaging life, in all its messiness and contradictoriness and complexity and hurt and pain, that we truly come to know love. The further we move from this full engagement, the closer we approach mere hedonism.

There is plenty of hedonism and escape elsewhere on *Born in the U.S.A.* as well. Repressed sexual longing saturates all two-and-a-half minutes (103 words total) of "I'm on Fire." One hopes, at the very least, that the woman to whom the song is addressed is only a metaphorical "little girl" left at home by her "daddy."

There is a more fully developed intimacy in "I'm Goin' Down," and the sexual tension here may exude less physical pain than in "I'm on Fire" (there are, at least, no references in this song to knife wounds in the soul). But once again, the title of the song indicates the trajectory of the characters' prospects, and the clarity with which Springsteen chronicles their relationship's descent would serve to remind us that in matters of the heart, sheer lust (and even physical compatibility) will only get you so far. Life lived on the surface of things grows vapid rather quickly, and when the characters have run out of things to talk about, the woman's "bored sighs" will rush in to fill the void. Where there were once the fires of passion, there are now only flashes of anger and recrimination.

Lost passion is the theme of "Dancing in the Dark" as well. Where the idea of dancing cheek-to-cheek with the one we love in a darkened room conjured up real romance in the 1930s song of the same name by Arthur Schwartz and Howard Dietz, in Springsteen's later version it merely represents a relationship that has reached its lowpoint. In that earlier song, the couple seems totally committed to one another—intent on being able to "face the music together." But in the song from *Born in the U.S.A.* we find yet another couple with nothing to say to each other. The man is "tired and bored" with himself; he looks to his partner for "a little help" in putting some fire back in their being together. He offers her his "gun" for hire, but she doesn't seem very interested in providing the "spark" he needs to light their fire again. Even the physicality in their relationship, it seems, has descended into dysfunction.

Where once the idea of "dancing in the dark" might have evoked images of candlelight romance and breathtaking intimacy, it now conjures up demons of frustration and failure. This couple is no longer *dancing* together at all. They are, rather, thrashing about in the darkness—fumbling for an exit, perhaps. Their relationship had probably been founded on material acquisitiveness, mere physicality, or similarly shifting sands. It should be no surprise to either of them that now their "little world" is "falling apart."

Lowering the Boom

Throughout his career, Springsteen has expressed anger about many of the iniquities inherent in modern society, and American society in particular. His characters—the marginalized Vietnam veteran, the out-of-work factory laborer, the disregarded employee at this or that dead-end job—are, as has been said, more often sinned against than sinning. They have often failed not because of any flaw within themselves, or even because they made particularly poor choices, but because an economic system favoring the already wealthy has stacked the deck against them.

This is not always the case, however. Some of Springsteen's characters in *Born in the U.S.A.* are, quite simply, *losers.* They may not have led the most privileged of lives. But at the end of the day (or by the end of the song), we know that they have no one but themselves to blame for their ultimate fall from grace. In a strange way, of course, hearing the absurd tales of their woe provides us with some sense of solace: for whatever *our* sins and failings, it is always nice to know that there are those even more obtuse than we are.

The amazing thing is that, oftentimes, people have no idea how bad their choices have been until the boom finally gets lowered. In both "Darlington County" and "Working on the Highway," the characters seem to be enjoying themselves—for the first half of the song, at least. But then, sooner or later, things fall apart.

Along with his friend Wayne, the narrator of "Darlington County" drives south from New York looking for work. The two end up in Darlington County, a rural area in northcentral South Carolina. There, with the help of Wayne's uncle, they hope to get union-scale construction jobs. They arrive in Darlington on the Fourth of July, and it's not long before they both hook up with a couple of local girls.

The narrator woos his "little girl standing on the corner" with all the (supposed) charm of a sophisticate from a northern metropolis. They're from New York City, he tells her, "big spenders" with all of "two hundred dollars" to blow. (Granted, there has been inflation since 1982, but that "two hundred dollars" still sounds similarly paltry to the "two grand" the narrator in "Meeting Across the River" was promised back in *Born to Run.*) Then, in words that became suddenly poignant in the wake of 9/11, he entices her with the declaration that "our pas each own one of the World Trade Centers"—and he promises her his towering edifice, for just "a kiss and a smile."

His entreaties seem to be successful, for by the start of the next verse—which is set seven days later—the girl is firmly ensconced in his front seat. But Wayne is nowhere to be seen, something that doesn't seem to aggrieve his pal too much, for he's already made plans to head farther south with his new sweetie. But as they drive out of Darlington County Wayne reemerges, handcuffed to the back of a police car.

The tone of "Working on the Highway" is (slightly) more serious, but the circumstances are strikingly similar. Perhaps the protagonist here is the same guy as in "Darlington County," having completed his foray further into Dixie and settled down as a regular member of a county road gang. All day this highway worker directs traffic and watches as hundreds, even thousands, of people speed off in different directions to somewhere else. But he doesn't travel anyplace; he just stands there, waving his flag, dreaming of leading "a better life than this" and finding that "pretty little miss" who will live for him alone, question nothing, do as she is told, and give him at least a modicum of earthly pleasure in this life.

He meets the one (he thinks) is the girl of his dreams at a dance one night. They get involved with one another. Perhaps she gets pregnant, but at any rate, they make plans to marry, and the prospective groom goes to meet his betrothed's father. This is when the boom gets lowered: she is a child, underage. "She's still a little girl," the father protests about his daughter, who knows nothing about making decisions as to her own future.

Again, as in "Darlington County," there is an attempt to flee farther south—to Florida this time. But the girl's brothers catch up with them; they take her back home to Georgia. The narrator is hauled off by the police and thrown in jail in the Sunshine State. As the song ends, he is still working on the highway, now as part of a chain gang—"blasting through the bedrock" as thick as his own dense skull.

Making Peace with the Past

Whatever the causes of their misfortune, *Born in the U.S.A.* has its share of the forlorn and dispossessed, of the marginalized and unsavory. But it also introduces us to a strikingly wide assortment of "normal" people like those among whom we all live and work. Springsteen admitted to feeling a good deal of ambivalence over many of the songs ultimately included on the album—songs that he felt veered too far over the line of rock into the pop category, or that veered too close to the blatantly commercial.[12] But there can be no doubt about the genuine affection he felt for many of the characters in these songs.

They, like most of us, are neither selfless saints nor unredeemable sinners. They are neither great heroes nor god-awful villains. They are, rather, like most of us—that is, people who do their best, who sometimes fail at what they attempt but who also sometimes manage to find joy and accomplishment in their lives and to touch the souls of others.

These characters are also men and women with particular histories. Each emerges as a product of a distinct set of relationships and influences. Just as we all inhabit our own present reality, so each one of us, too, has a past—which both blesses and curses us, and which, in many cases, shadows us as we emerge into the present.

Springsteen had written the largely autobiographical song "No Surrender" as a remembrance of his earlier years growing up in New Jersey, especially of his relationship with his bandmate Steven Van Zandt. Originally, Springsteen had not wanted to include it on *Born in the U.S.A.* and for many years continued to express doubts that the song belonged there. But at the "eleventh hour," Springsteen said later, Van Zandt had convinced him to include it.[13]

The first verse of "No Surrender" presents an energetic portrait of adolescent bravado: members of the adult world are derided as "those fools"; school is useless; liberation comes when the bandmates manage to "bust" out of class (as one would "bust" out of a jail) and follow the call of the beating drum to the only school of real freedom and true wisdom—the school of rock and roll.

Then there is the covenant: the bandmates form a pact and promise always to honor their bond with one another (and with the liberating power of their music). "No retreat, baby, no surrender," the chorus reiterates.

Such pledges come easily to the young. Time, like an ever-flowing stream, soon bears them all away. By the next line, the years have taken their toll; there is sadness and aging, and passions have dimmed. Yet something of that earlier spirit abides: if we cannot physically "grow young again," then at least the rock and roll promise—its perennially youthful attitude—holds something of time's toll at bay.

"No Surrender" begins in the past but ends in the present. By its last, more introspective, verse, the perspective has shifted from that of a rebellious adolescent with the world to win, to that of a tired adult who feels that his world has grown too small. His energy has grown too weak to transcend life's limitations any longer, and he leaves it to others now to continue the battle that rages outside his bedroom window. God offers to everyone the choice between truth and repose, Emerson once said. In the way we live our lives, we choose one or the other—but we can never have both. The narrator of "No Surrender" seems to have chosen the latter, at least physically. It is time now for him to rest.

But still, in his mind at least, the wide horizon's grander view still beckons, and his "romantic dreams" still abide. "No Surrender" speaks to that spirit within all of us which refuses to let dreams die, that spirit which refuses to grow "sad and old" in spite of the passage of time and the torments of daily existence.

"Bobby Jean" is also a song that looks backward. It, too, deals with Springsteen's days as a teenager back in New Jersey, and more particularly once again with his relationship with Steve Van Zandt. Friends since their teenage years, Springsteen and Van Zandt played in various bands together on the Jersey Shore, and from the time of *Born to Run* Van Zandt had been an important influence on Springsteen, as well as a member of the E Street Band. While work was continuing on the *Born in the U.S.A.* album, Van Zandt told Springsteen of his desire to leave the band in order to pursue various musical projects on his own. "Bobby Jean" is generally heard as Springsteen's farewell to his old bandmate.

As Bruce counts time, and the beat of what could be a simple garage band swells in the background, Springsteen tells of stopping by the house of his friend, only to be told by her mother that she's left. The singer seems surprised by the news, and somewhat regretful, though not especially angry. Sometimes life simply changes more quickly than we anticipate, and there's no way to prepare for the change. We just have to accept it and move on.

But if we have been blessed by a real friendship with someone, there will always be those memories to remind us just how important that relationship has been. The singer recollects all the ways that Bobby Jean has touched his life, "ever since we were sixteen." She has provided the unshakable loyalty of a friend who accepted him as he was, regardless of what others said. They have shared together the mutual joy of common pleasures and shared opinions—not least, their shared opinion of one another—as so far superior to the lesser souls around them. There was in their relationship, too, the deepest of all manifestations of friendship: the sharing of one being with another and the articulation of feelings that one would not feel safe expressing to anyone else—an open voicing of all those hurts one hides from all the world, except one's friends. When our friend is gone, it is as though a part of us has been taken, too; we doubt whether anyone will ever be able to replace that old companion.

But at least as a musician Springsteen has some recourse. He can cast his bittersweet ode to friendship as a song and hope that fate will allow his friend to hear it someday, as she continues down her own road and goes about her own business. Perhaps something will stir in her a memory of this friendship that they have shared, and in that memory she will know at last the singer's deep gratitude toward her for having blessed his life with such kindness.

The memories we have can either warm our hearts or torment us. Often, memories of the same situation can affect different people in different ways. "Glory Days" begins with a memory of a friend from high school who was a star baseball pitcher. Back then he was on top of the heap: feared for his athletic prowess, honored for being at the top of his class. Now, upon meeting him in a barroom one night, the singer learns that the guy is stuck in the old days. His only reality is what he *did.* The present holds no honor or glory for him; indeed, it offers him no real life worth talking about.

There's another member of that high school class the singer knows—somewhat more intimately, we might guess. Life has not been especially kind to this woman: divorced from her husband a couple of years ago, she now faces life as a single mother—never an easy row to hoe. But the same past that has handcuffed the ex-baseball player is one of those few things that provides this harried mom a bit of pleasure in her life. She enjoys remembering the past, but she doesn't seek to dwell there any longer. That's because the life she leads *now*—as imperfect as it certainly is—offers treasures more genuine than any phantasms of herself as a beauty queen. She has children who love her and need her; she has a new mate with whom she can enjoy simple good times. Her life is unremarkable, certainly. But there is within it enough goodness—and enough real living—to uplift her spirit and keep her on the road to the future.

You Can Go Home Again

"My Hometown" brings the album to its close and serves as the appropriate final complement to "Born in the U.S.A.," the song with which the album began. Indeed, the main character in "My Hometown" was also born in the U.S.A.—as were all the characters on the record, for that matter. He was born thirty-five years before, in the very same town from which he now sings.

The first memory he shares is a simple domestic incident from when he was eight years old: running to get a ten-cent newspaper for his father from the bus stop at the corner. Then he remembers sitting on his father's lap, steering their Buick through the streets of the place where they live. "This is your hometown," his father tells him. It is an unambiguous statement of pride, reflecting their shared roots, their hopes, and their love for one another.

But then bad times invade their city, and Springsteen makes an unmistakable allusion here to the race riots that shattered his adopted hometown, Asbury Park, in the 1960s. After this racial violence, the town's descent only accelerates: businesses leave, factories close, people lose their jobs. Many families move away, but others stick it out. This is the choice faced by the song's narrator and his wife as they lie in bed at night discussing their future: What is the best choice they can make for themselves—but even more importantly, for their young son? Do they stay in this place which has been their home for all their lives, or do they move south, where their economic prospects, at least, might be somewhat better? Do they try to give their son a more comfortable life, or do they tough it out and give him something more: a sense of belonging, a sense of community, some awareness of rootedness and his connection with those who have come before?

Certainly, the popular choice in those years of Reaganomics and supply-side determinism would have been to follow the financial goad and forget about such sentimental vestiges as "home" or "community." In a world economy, the powers that be might tell us, we have no "hometowns" any longer.

But what does it profit a man if he gains the whole world and loses his own soul? In the end, the narrator chooses belonging over accumulating, and the certainties of his hometown (not necessarily the most attractive certainties) over the possibilities (and possibly better prospects) of somewhere else. It is no easy decision for anyone to make—and a strikingly countercultural one, given the time and place in which he lives.

But as he puts his son on his own lap, as his father did twenty-seven years before to him, he introduces the boy, too, to this hometown—*their* hometown—this unremarkable place where their people have lived and died down through the generations. His feelings about this place may not be as unambiguously positive as were those of the generations that came before him. But as he reenacts this ritual of connection, he initiates his son to the bond they share, and the circle becomes full. He has kept faith with those who have come before—kept faith with his forefathers and foremothers who have worked so hard—and in doing so, he has kept faith with the living essence of this dream that is called America.

Chapter Eight

Overcoming the Long Loneliness

Tunnel of Love, Human Touch, Lucky Town

It would have been extremely challenging under any circumstances for Springsteen to duplicate the wanton commercial success of *Born in the U.S.A.* The album had raced to the top of the
charts and eventually sold something over 15 million copies. It had
spawned *seven* Top 10 singles; a feat that only Michael Jackson's
Thriller had done before (in 1983) and that Janet Jackson's *Rhythm
Nation 1814* would do afterward (in 1990).[1] For sixteen months—
between June 1984 and October 1985—the band had toured the
world, playing more than 150 shows before a total audience of over
four million people (with total ticket sales of over $100 million).[2]

Springsteen had no illusions that his subsequent works could
ever match those statistics. There was not going to be another
mainstream rock album blatantly loaded with Top 10 hits, at least
not right away. Springsteen allowed Columbia to release a five-
record live set in November 1986, *Bruce Springsteen and the E
Street Band Live/1975–85.* The five records of *Live* contained forty
tracks, spanning concert performances from the band's entire
career. Released in time for the 1986 Christmas shopping season,
the set debuted on the record charts at number one, and went on to
become the best-selling live album up to that time.[3] But by the fall
of 1986, with megastardom now achieved and with the worldwide
tour for *Born in the U.S.A.* finally completed, Springsteen once
again retreated back into his home recording studio (now set up
above his garage in Rumson, New Jersey). "I really enjoyed the

success of *USA,*" he said later, "but by the end of that whole thing I was kind of 'Bruced' out. I was like, 'Whoa, enough of that.' "[4]

A few months before the end of the *Born in the U.S.A.* tour, Springsteen had wed the actress Julianne Phillips, on her twenty-fifth birthday, May 13, 1985. Increasingly over the next year or so, as Springsteen spent more time with Phillips—as well as with Jon Landau and recording engineer Chuck Plotkin—he and the band drifted apart. They seldom spoke among themselves, much less made music together. In time, too, Springsteen's relationship with Phillips also cooled. The songs he began recording at home in Rumson increasingly chronicled the deterioration of a relationship.

The album that resulted from these recording sessions, *Tunnel of Love,* was released in October 1987. *Tunnel of Love* was basically a solo effort: the E Street Band was named on the liner notes, but contributed little to it musically. Springsteen had recorded much of the music himself, using drum machines and synthesizers. However, he and the band were reunited early in 1988 for the "*Tunnel of Love* Express"—a six-month tour that would take them across the country and back to Europe. In Rome that June, paparazzi snapped Bruce in his nightshirt, out on a hotel balcony with a similarly clad Patti Scialfa, a backup singer in the band.[5] By the end of the summer, Phillips had filed for divorce, and the marriage officially ended in March 1989.

It was an emotionally difficult time for all involved. In September 1988, Springsteen joined a half dozen other major acts for the six-week Human Rights Now! Tour sponsored by Amnesty International. When the tour was over he returned to Rumson for a bit of rest. There he poured out his conflicted emotions onto the pages of his notebooks and then onto tape in his home studio. About a year later, in October 1989, the E Street Band was officially disbanded, and Bruce and Patti began spending almost all of their time on the West Coast, at the multimillion-dollar estate Springsteen had purchased in Beverly Hills. Their first child, Evan James Springsteen, was born in California in July 1990; within three-and-a-half years, the couple would also have a daughter (Jessica Ray) and another son (Sam Ryan). In June 1991, Springsteen and

Scialfa were married in a civil ceremony in Los Angeles. All the while, Bruce continued to write more songs about the trepidations—and joys—of human relationships.

Two additional record albums emerged from this cauldron of emotional highs and lows, both released on the very same day, March 31, 1992. The first of the two new albums, *Human Touch,* was the result of work Springsteen had done with a new group of musicians in California. "*Human Touch* began as an exercise to get myself back into writing and recording," Springsteen said.[6] He had written a variety of songs in different genres—soul, rock, pop, R&B. Now it was time to see how they sounded on record. Arduously, Springsteen had worked his way through the vast archive of material he had produced, including a few songs he had cowritten with his bandmate Roy Bittan. Finally, he selected fourteen songs, all loosely grouped around a common theme that Springsteen described as people's need "to surrender themselves to each other and accept fate."[7]

Once the material on *Human Touch* was completed, Springsteen continued to write largely autobiographical songs dealing with all he had been through over the past few years. The birth of his son had given rise to the song "Living Proof," which in turn gave rise to more songs about his relationship with Patti, their marriage, and the hopes and fears he had for the future. Things moved very quickly, and within three weeks, Springsteen had recorded an entire new album, *Lucky Town.*

Neither *Human Touch* nor the somewhat more critically respected *Lucky Town* turned out to be a huge commercial success, at least compared to Springsteen's more recent works.[8] Considered together, they constitute Bruce Springsteen's declaration of his full immersion into domestic life, with all of the deep regrets, cavernous sorrows, and soul-shaking inspiration such engagement represents.

Just a Little of That Human Touch

The great Catholic social activist Dorothy Day often spoke of what she called the "long loneliness"—that deep, inner emptiness within us that only love can fill. Prior to his marriage to Julianne

Phillips in 1985, Springsteen had seemed at times to be searching almost feverishly to find that one total and committed relationship that would help him transcend his sense of utter aloneness and personal isolation. While he was still unmarried well into his thirties, his "freedom" had its costs. Because Springsteen was spending more and more time alone in the studio, his circle of friends was growing progressively smaller. If he was ever going to "settle down" (whatever that meant, given the peripatetic life he led as a world celebrity) and father children, it would have to be sometime soon. As one of his songs on *Tunnel of Love* stated, "When you're alone you ain't nothing but alone." Increasingly, Springsteen came to discern that aloneness, in and of itself, does not equal freedom. One could have "the fortunes of heaven in diamonds and gold," as well as that entire delectable catalogue of earthly pleasures and honors enumerated in "Ain't Got You." But without the one thing that was missing—that deepest of human relationships—one could still be a forlorn soul.

But if, as Augustine said, to know another person deeply is to know God, then letting that other inside oneself is also the most profound step on the road to self-knowledge. Allowing someone inside one's psychic and emotional boundaries is never easy, and can be a profound challenge for one who has kept the self walled off for as long, perhaps, as Springsteen had.

Given the pace of intimacy in the modern world, often the first line of defense to be broached between two people is the physical. Often in a culture of narcissism, where the body is commercialized and sexuality trivialized, the penetration of the physical boundary becomes an end in itself, an act of "conquest" as it were. However, in the generation of genuine intimacy—intimacy between two complete beings, in all aspects of their personhood—the physical meeting serves not as an end but as a means, as the bridge toward this deeper knowing.

Among some African tribes, it is said that all people experience "two hungers." The first is for food and those things that sustain life; the second (and greater) is for a sense of purpose and meaning and intimacy. As Bruce himself had sung back in 1979, "Everybody's got a hungry heart."

But often some physical means is needed to feed this deeper hunger of the heart. We yearn to be rescued from this "world without pity"—this world grown too fast and cold and inhumane—through that genuine "human touch": by a touching of hands, a communion of physical beings, a sharing of deepest selves. The sparks which this deep personal communion can generate can illuminate our spirits and set these pent-up hearts of ours to beating once again.

This is no meeting of saints, certainly. No one of us is anybody's "bargain"; we all come into relationships with a full array of scrapes and dents, issues and hurts; we're all broken in some way. But most of our faults and imperfections aren't fatal; they can be repaired and need simply "a little touchup and a little paint"—a little self-care or a little attention from the hands of one we care about.

In continuing to avoid the depths and challenges of such intimate relationships, we cling for dear life to that "safety [we] prize." We seek to maintain full control over how we spend our days and live our lives. But ultimately, playing it safe and maintaining our aloofness disengages us from life. We grow hard and cold—dehumanized. We become "pretenders," pretending to live according to the script we have written in our heads rather than really living, while all the while, real life—with all its "risk and pain" but with all of its genuine love, too—slips away and passes us by.

Often, however, propelled by our loneliness perhaps, we finally stop waiting for supernatural, miraculous intervention and make our move toward another. There will be no manna falling from heaven, no miracle of wine and blood this time. We're going to find "no miracles here," Springsteen sings. Nothing will change unless we break out of our self-imposed isolation and reach out to the other.

Then, in reaching out, we'll discover that it's "just you and me tonight": the two of us against the world, in a sense, but the two of us also joined in this life, together—"riders on this train" which is this world, which is this life. In the human touch we exchange with each other, our arms and bodies and lives become intertwined with one another. We cling together and give each other something to which to cling; we provide for each other some support and comfort to get us through this life.

It Takes a Leap of Faith

When we finally manage to get out of our ruts of self-sufficiency and the need to control, and then do what we must to reach out to that other person, we may discover those precious gifts that separate being offers to us. But this is seldom an easy move to make, and breaking with past habits can be threatening.

In "Cautious Man" from *Tunnel of Love,* Springsteen introduces us to someone who proves able to make such a change in his life, but for whom the process of change is painfully difficult.

Bill Horton is the "cautious man" of the song's title. He had lived the greater part of his life with great care. Sticking strictly to his code of conduct, he was ever prudent in his enterprises, always carefully appraising the situation he was in, measuring his life—if not in coffee spoons like T. S. Eliot's Prufrock—then with the tape measure and level of a carefully trained handyman who likes his lines straight and his contours predictable.

But Bill has the sense at least to let his "cautiousness slip away" enough to follow love's call when he hears it. He falls in love with a young woman, marries her, settles down, and strives to be as good a man married as he was when he was by himself. But the sharing of his life with another has opened the door to risk, and Bill now fears all the possible grief this new relationship might bring. Indeed, in opening the door of his life fully to *love*, he opens it fully to *fear* as well. Love and fear now vie with each other to become the guiding impetus of his life (we are told that he has even tattooed those two words, one on each hand).

As these conflicting emotions struggle within him, Bill prays for guidance and the strength to remain stable. Finally, one night, the tension between love and fear comes to a head. His dreams are haunted with dark possibilities, a sense of dread that will not leave him. This fear threatens to extinguish the love that he still feels (deeply) for the woman to whom he has dedicated his life.

But even while his demons haunt him, his wife sleeps, peaceful and unaffected by his torment. In the depths of the night, he stares down the long highway and knows that, whatever fears might accompany him, he must continue down the road of his life.

Bill knows that there will be no final vanquishing here, no ultimate resolution. But as the moon smiles its benediction upon him, Bill ponders his young wife's face bathed "with the beauty of God's fallen light." He knows now, in this holy moment at least, that love abides and that (for now at least) that love is enough to cast out all fear.

Sometimes when we arrive at the point of reaching out, it is the other one who pulls us into the new reality we have to face. Once grabbed by the allure of that person's presence, we know that the time has come to commit. Sometimes, as Springsteen sings, "it takes a leap of faith" for us to move to a deeper relationship.

In "Leap of Faith" the physical body of another is the bridge toward something deeper. Knowing a person physically can lead to our knowing that person in a deeply emotional and even spiritual sense. "Leap of Faith" presents images of the body of the other as sacramental: the woman's legs are likened to "heaven," her breasts to "the altar," and her entire body becomes "the holy land." The song goes on to allude, with little subtlety, to a sexual encounter, and Springsteen pronounces himself "sanctified" by the entire experience.

Human lovemaking reminds us that, however old and life-worn we might be, we are still alive; that in spite of the passing of the years, we can feel eternally young in that moment of deep sharing. In taking that leap of faith, we are born again to a new being where two become one.

Tougher than the Rest

It takes more than physical consummation to guarantee that a relationship will have a chance to survive in this hard world. It takes commitment. It takes dedication. It takes people who are, as Springsteen says, "Tougher than the Rest." The road of life is often dark, and there is oftentimes only "a thin thin line" dividing whatever partial victories we achieve in this life from defeat. Romantic fantasies and the easy pleasures they promise might entice and excite. But those who might seem "handsome" or "good-lookin' " or "sweet-talkin' " often don't last. By morning they're gone, and one is left to face the struggles and roughness of life alone. For a lifetime partner, one needs someone who is tougher than these run-of-the-mill lovers, one who is "tougher than the rest."

This is the person who offers his commitment on a lifetime basis. He'll walk that "thin line"—that treacherous tightrope between success and failure—for you and with you, anytime and every time you need him. He is not perfect, certainly; he comes with baggage, with issues—as do we all. There is nothing flawless or airbrushed about him. But your relationship together is "another dance," representing a new day and the new hopes love can bring if you dare to hope and dare to engage in this dance of life.

It's a rough and tough dance sometimes. In this "Real World" we often find that it's no well-meaning stranger but a "Mister Trouble" who comes walking our way and accompanies us down this road of life. This trouble may sometimes be the result of our own poor decisions, and we may build within our hearts an ugly "shrine" made out of the "fool's gold" of bitter memories and self-pity.

But even if we come to experience our lives as the sad and garish "roadside carnival" described in "Real World," at least we might take some consolation in the fact that, wounded as we are, we're still alive. The final verdict on our life has yet to be delivered. Just because the past has been miserable doesn't mean the future has to be as well. Faith abides that there might still be that "one clear moment of love and truth" out there somewhere—that moment when the "real world" appears as it truly is. It's not heroic or romantic (there will be no bells ringing, no flags waving in the breeze). But life for us still has the possibility to be *real* and awake, with "arms open wide" to both the joys and the sorrows that a fully lived life will bring.

And there can be no doubt that it will bring both. "Joy and woe are woven fine," wrote William Blake, "clothing for the soul divine." In another song on *Human Touch,* Springsteen likens life to a "Roll of the Dice." The crap shooter may have a long string of losing throws, but this will never stop him from believing that maybe the next roll of the dice will bring him "elevens and sevens" at last.

Perhaps we are dwelling in a "fool's paradise" if we cling to this hope and go on trying. The odds of finding happiness aren't always in our favor. But hope reminds us that, whatever life has brought us in the past, it is possible to live in relationships where we love one another. Hope opens our eyes to life in all of its dimensions, all of its sadness and pain, all of its emptiness and despair, and all of its glory, beauty, and love. Hope keeps us afloat when otherwise life would drown us. It shows us life in all its fullness and has the courage to ask us the question, "How dare we let go?"

But hope also reminds us that it is not enough to cling. It is not enough to drift passively through life. Hope is not passive; it means active engagement in life. There is a responsibility of hope, a responsibility that often comes only with one's full entry into adulthood and full commitment to its demands. Nurturing and caring for another human soul "ain't for one of the boys," Springsteen sings in "Man's Job," also on *Human Touch*. "Loving you woman is a man's man's job," he sings heartily. Love is a full-time job; indeed, it's a full-life job. And, as yet another song on *Human Touch* indicates, it takes a "Real Man" to do it: "Well, you can beat on your chest," and think you're a man, Springsteen sings. But "Hell, any monkey can" do as much as that. Real masculinity isn't about noise and bravado or merely exercising power over another. Real masculinity is open to the wide range of emotions love engenders. It's about letting go of control long enough to make a commitment and render care for another. It's coming to the realization that meeting our responsibilities is the price we pay for the gift of life we have been given.

Down into the Tunnel

But nothing is preordained. Even when we find the one we've been searching for and make a commitment, there will be plenty of dangers, toils, and snares along the way. Sometimes, seemingly inexplicably, love's highway veers off the sun-warmed pathways and descends into a dark and frightening "Tunnel of Love." The ticket-taker may whisper "Good luck" to us as we descend but basing a relationship on chance offers none of the firmness that commitment brings. A garish carnival ride does not a lifelong journey make, nor is a "little fun house" the hard-won, well-built loving edifice required to shelter a deep and intimate relationship.

So as the car descends into the tunnel and it grows dark, we are left alone with our deepest fears. Staggering about in the darkness, fake mirrors and artificial lighting present a tawdry portrait of each to the other. They grow uncertain about who they truly are; uncomprehending of the other, they become strangers.

What might have seemed like a facile enough journey at the start—"Man meets a woman and they fall in love"—has now degenerated into either a pitched battle or a ridiculous spectacle. Romance can be easy; it's real life that's hard. Without a whole array of spiritual gifts—tenacity, forbearance, patience, among others—this man and woman, however decent each might be individually, will never be able to vanquish the ghosts that haunt their being together.

Their life will become stuck in neutral. There will be no fire or warmth left in it—like the furnace that won't work or the engine that won't start in the song "One Step Up." The only heat they generate now arises from the arguments and fights of the "dirty little war" they're now fighting. Every day they lose a little bit of ground—they take "one step up and two steps back," until finally theirs becomes just another failed marriage. For this sad pair, their days together have become little more than (as the title of another song indicates) "The Long Goodbye."

Becoming Strangers

Why do so many relationships in general, and marriages in particular, fail? There are many possible reasons, and a specific combination of factors plays its part in each particular failure. But one leading reason Springsteen explores in these three relationship-centered albums is the corrosive effect of a lack of honesty.

Sometimes people continue to play the dating game past the courtship and into the marriage. Each partner wears a "brilliant disguise" to impress the other. But then, even when the courtship is over and the marriage is pronounced, the disguises stay on. A man or woman thrilled by the prospect of romance might find the "mystery" of his or her prospective partner enticing and alluring. But once a couple is married, communication has to take the place of mystery. Amid the day-to-day challenges of domestic life, it hardly seems prudent to have to read someone's mind in order to know what he or she is really thinking.

Sometimes, perhaps, it's not so much a case of a relationship "falling apart" as it is the light of day finally providing a hard and honest second look, exposing everything that was lacking in the first place. In time, perhaps, the actors change their costumes: the "brilliant disguise" of the infatuated couple before marriage becomes the camouflage of the "loving woman" and the "faithful man" after the vows are repeated. But if both are still more interested in maintaining their disguises than in truly opening up to one another and sharing life honestly, then ultimately each is in the game to benefit himself or herself alone.

No amount of good intentions or high sounding verbiage or even hard work can salvage a relationship where honesty and truthfulness do not abide. Too often the lies (either personal or societal) that we have told or have bought into—and the hatred and spite that we have cultivated within our souls and in our lives—pull us down. Once we allow duplicity to guide us, we "start out standing but end up crawlin,'" Springsteen sings in "The Big Muddy." A life—or a society—built on the shifting sands of lies will end up collapsing sooner or later. Or, when we insist on wearing "Two Faces," we end up hiding not only from those around us but from our own selves as well.

Better Days Shining Through

There are those losses in life that can beat the hell out of us. Faced with paying such great cost, we might well question whether it is even worthwhile going on with life and whether we will ever again feel a sense of rightness with the world. But the human spirit is stronger than any force that can be mustered against it. "Such is life," the Buddha once intoned, "seven times down and eight times up."

"The only way out is through," another adage goes. Sometimes when we pass through the dark night of the soul, we discover there really can be the bright dawn of a new day on the other side. Certainly this is what Springsteen himself experienced as he lived through the deterioration of one marriage and the budding and flowering of another.

"Better Days" is the first song on the *Lucky Town* album and serves as a sort of bridge between these two stages in Springsteen's life. *Lucky Town* may be the most explicitly autobiographical of Springsteen's albums: fully eight of the album's ten songs deal, to one degree or another, with his relationship with Patti Scialfa, their marriage, or the birth of their first child.[9]

At the beginning of "Better Days," Springsteen is still mourning the death of his relationship with Julianne Phillips. He's empty, soulless, waiting for his "life to begin." But with the arrival of his "pretty red rose" (Scialfa), "better days" have finally arrived and he has found the woman with whom he truly wants to share his life.

Without her love, his life had grown hard and cold. In spite of his wealth and success, life was unsatisfying. He was like a man spitting in the face of fortune, a rich man (both in terms of wealth and opportunity) pretending to be poor (both in terms of money and spirit). The lack of love in his life caused him to view everything through dark-colored spectacles. Now, with the new arrival of love, even his "hard luck bones" are being transformed into blessings.

"Better days" have arrived, Springsteen sings again and again. With these better days and this new love must come, too, a new attitude, a new way of looking at life. There will be no more complaining in the face of life's blessedness, no more self-pity for one to whom life has given so much. He is barely over his hurt, but he is already "halfway to heaven" too—well on the way to becoming the fully responsible, fully alive human being God intends him to be.

Following quickly on the heals of "Better Days" comes "Lucky Town," which also ponders the passing of the years and how the angle from which we look at something changes it completely.

"Lucky Town" refers more to a frame of mind than a specific

geographical place. Wherever we are, the years make their demands upon us. Life can start feeling too crowded, but the sky above is clear, and the air has been cleansed by the hard rain that has fallen. If one listens closely, one can hear voices calling out that it's time to move on. Hope is in the air.

It wasn't always thus: before this transformation, the singer thought that even life's choicest gifts had flaws in them; even the finest set of clothes he owned had a string dangling down, threatening to unravel the whole wardrobe. But, when he followed that dangling thread, it lead somehow to the home of his beloved—to this fortunate place, this Lucky Town, that had been blocked from sight before.

Building a new edifice of the spirit won't be easy. The dirt on our hands never comes off, and there may be wounds that will never heal. But the labor will be worth the effort, for the "new home" that is being built here will be a temple not just of luck but of love, not just of toil but of joy.

The Great Circle of Family

There is more than a little irony, perhaps, that the most lighthearted song amid the emotional baggage of *Tunnel of Love* deals with Springsteen's relationship with his father. Springsteen had touched upon their tumultuous relationship often in the past, both in songs (most directly, perhaps, in "Independence Day" on *The River*), as well as in numerous concert monologues. Theirs was not an easy bond, certainly. "We'd always end up screamin' at each other," Springsteen told Dave Marsh in 1979, adding that his arguments with his father sometimes even led to physical altercations.[10]

By the time of "Walk Like a Man," however, maturity seems to have afforded a truce. The father with whom he had been so often at loggerheads—for whom in his songs he had expressed as much pity as regard—now emerges as friend, confidant, and mentor.

In the song, Springsteen remembers his father on the day of his wedding: both strong (with rough, manly hands) and vulnerable (weeping on his son's shoulder). The experience conjures up in

Bruce an early childhood memory of trying to walk in his father's footsteps—literally—over a sandy New Jersey beach. He was too small back then to match such a manly stride. Now, accompanied by his father to the marriage altar, he imitates again his steps into matrimony and perhaps into full manhood—and all the mystery and uncertainty that represents.

He is now his own man at last, Springsteen affirms: an independent human being, now fully responsible for his own decisions. In a sense, he is no longer his father's child. He has emerged at last out from under his father's shadow, and his father's demons no longer haunt him (for he will have his own to face in due time). He understands now that the best way he can honor his father is by taking care to leave his own footprints, firm and strong and bold, in the sands of time over which he will now travel.

The clearest evidence any of us leaves of our having been here in this world is, of course, the bearing and nurturing of children. In the song "Living Proof," Springsteen meditates on the birth of his first child, Evan James (born on July 25, 1990).

Springsteen believes that every child is a reflection of the divine, holy in his or her essence—"a little piece of the Lord's undying light." Standing before the cradle of his first son, he is overcome by the child's power and beauty; the experience gives him a sense of connection with the Divine he had never felt before. It provides for him the "missing words" of his life's prayer, the missing component needed to complete and fulfill his humanity. This "fouled and confused" world has repeatedly sullied him, and bruised him, and angered him. But now he knows at last there is meaning and purpose at the very heart of human existence. The birth of his child is "living proof" that God's mercy beats at the very heart of creation.

Now Springsteen feels as though his life has been redeemed. He is no longer disengaged from life; the darkness has been lifted; he doesn't have to run from who he is any longer. Life is fragile, he understands—as fragile as a newborn child, and just as precious. The birth of every child, it has been said, is evidence that God hasn't given up on humanity. This realization pierces Springsteen's heart as he watches his son sleep. After a long period of spiritual drought, he feels bathed in grace once again.

During this period, there was also developing within Springsteen the growing realization that we are not only responsible for our own children, our own direct progeny, but for *all* children—especially, perhaps, for those without adequate support and protection. In "Souls of the Departed" from *Lucky Town*, he laments those who have died before their time, leaving behind brokenhearted and bereft loved ones.

He sings of a young man named Lieutenant Jimmy Bly, stationed in Iraq during the Gulf War of 1990–1991. Bly has drawn the unenviable duty of sorting through the clothes of his dead comrades. He seems haunted by their presence as he goes about his work. The second character in "Souls of the Departed" is Raphael Rodriguez, a seven-year-old child in California, gunned down in an act of gang violence. His mother mourns him intensely; the rest of the world seems unconcerned.

In this song, Springsteen views the violence of the world in the light of his new experience as a father. He now knows firsthand how precious life is, and he empathizes with those who have lost the ones they loved. Yet his initial impulse in wanting to protect his family is to withdraw, to "build me a wall" around the well-manicured life he has built for himself.

But as the song draws to a close he senses that such withdrawal—from the problems of the world, from the ethical standards he says he affirms—does not succeed in making the world a better or safer place. It does not keep faith with those who have been taken. It does not provide an adequate or honest response to the prayer the song utters. Springsteen infers that only a life lived honestly and compassionately—only a life that does not turn its eyes from the world's problems—honors the souls of those who have departed.

Two Become One

It's a hard-won romance that permeates these three albums and that comes to fullest flower, perhaps, with *Lucky Town*. Indeed, while *Tunnel of Love* displays an overall balance between hope and despair (think of the two words "love" and "fear" tattooed across the knuckles of the main character in "Cautious Man"), and while *Human Touch* lumbers pretty much in the throes of despair (rising on occasion at least to its heights of cynicism), with *Lucky Town* Springsteen is writing as a man who still vividly remembers the magic and joy of his wedding day.

Certainly the wooing had begun sometime before. "All That Heaven Will Allow" on *Tunnel of Love* exulted in the possibilities of finding at least some glory and energy in the man-woman relationship. Our love for that one special person, when it is reciprocated, is as close to heaven as we get in this life, Springsteen sings. It banishes the clouds of life and transcends its storms and darkness. Adversity doesn't matter when you've found the woman who loves you and "who wants to wear your ring." Even "Valentine's Day" (also from *Tunnel of Love*), for all its imagery of driving a car down a dark highway and dying in bed, preaches the ennobling and inspiring powers of love.

But with *Lucky Town,* the marriage is a done deal. In its final song, "My Beautiful Reward," Springsteen looks back and retells how he and the woman he loves finally arrived at where they now blessedly find themselves. Brutally honest, it contains plenty of self-loathing about what a jerk he had been in the years just previous, but by the final verse, he has risen above his folly like a phoenix and now soars over the "gray fields" of life.

But *Lucky Town* is largely free of such recrimination. Instead, we're either invited to join in the celebration and witness the wedding ceremony itself, or we're invited to look forward beyond the wedding and contemplate where the union of this man and this woman will lead.

"Book of Dreams" is a series of musical snapshots from the reception that followed the wedding ceremony uniting Springsteen and Scialfa in 1991. Reviewing these simple scenes in his mind (in his dreams?), Springsteen senses their power: they are the simple strands from which the fabric of his new life will be woven. Bathed now in the soft light of moon and stars, they seem, in memory at least, to be enchanted. The love they represent is, indeed, holy; it's part of the timeless web of all creation; it shimmers with beauty and mystery. If nothing can protect these lovers from the dangers life might bring, their dance together is nevertheless blessed, and together they represent an infinitely more powerful force than either would have been alone.

"If I Should Fall Behind" ponders both the journey that has brought these two people to this point in their lives and the road that will follow their exchange of vows. It speaks primarily of the power of commitment. Even when two people love each other, life can be difficult. When things grow dark and the twilight falls, we can grow confused. Our individual steps "fall so differently" from those of another, sometimes one or the other of us might "fall behind." There will always be those expected differences between two people, in temperament or outlook or upbringing. While such differences are hardly unusual, they can nevertheless add stress to a relationship. We dream of that perfect love "lasting and true," but we know how life buffets us and wears us out sometimes. We know there is always the danger that we might grow apart from each other.

But the vows we repeat in marriage are a symbol of our living commitment. They cannot endure unless we make them endure. Spoken vows have no hidden or magical power in and of themselves, but we have the power—through our commitment to each other in every step we take together—to make our vows real and true and even eternal.

Beneath the boughs of a sturdy and deeply rooted oak tree, by the side of a river that flows steadily onward, a couple pledges that they will honor and cherish one another 'til death do them part. But even after death parts them—even after they "lose each other" as the shadows of night fall over them—their love will remain and their commitment will abide. They will dance together through all eternity, forever, as Gibran said, "in the silent memory of God."

Chapter Nine

Seeking Justice

The Ghost of Tom Joad

*A*fter the simultaneous release of *Human Touch* and *Lucky Town*, it would be nearly three years until another album by Bruce Springsteen would appear. Early in 1995, Springsteen had reassembled the full E Street Band to record several new songs for his *Greatest Hits* collection.[1] The band played together for only a week at the Hit Factory in New York, where Springsteen had previously recorded most of *Born in the U.S.A.* Over that single week, Springsteen and the band recorded together about a half dozen songs, of which "Secret Garden," "Blood Brothers," and an updated version of "This Hard Land" were included with earlier material on the *Greatest Hits* record. The next month the band got together once again, briefly, for a live performance of "Murder Incorporated," which was also included in the album's lineup.[2]

Among the songs that hadn't made the cut for the *Greatest Hits* compendium was a new work Springsteen had written called "The Ghost of Tom Joad." As with many of the songs on the earlier *Nebraska* album, "Tom Joad" seemed to sound more intense and direct when Springsteen sang it solo, accompanied only by himself on guitar and harmonica, than when backed by the full band. When the full-band arrangement of the song failed to catch fire, Springsteen put it aside and went on to the next piece.

Nobody's Kiddin' Nobody

Springsteen was inspired to write "The Ghost of Tom Joad" by director John Ford's adaptation of *The Grapes of Wrath* by John Steinbeck. Steinbeck's novel, published in 1939, centers on a sharecropper from Oklahoma, Tom Joad, who sets out for California with his family in the midst of the Great Depression. From 1930 onward thousands of destitute men, women, and children migrated from the Dust Bowl of the Great Plains to California, hoping for a better life out west. In awarding the 1962 Nobel Prize for literature to Steinbeck, the Nobel committee called *The Grapes of Wrath* "a poignant description of the experiences of one particular farmer and his family during their endless, heartbreaking journey to a new home."[3]

Springsteen seems to have been moved by the rich characterization of Steinbeck's (and Ford's) work. He also identified with the impetus within 1930s' social activism to speak on behalf of the destitute and disenfranchised. Certainly, this spirit of solidarity with the dowtrodden was nothing new for Springsteen. It had characterized many of the songs on *Darkness on the Edge of Town* and *Nebraska*. His craving for social justice had also involved him in a number of high profile causes. In early 1985, Springsteen had joined the ranks of musical stars who comprised USA for Africa. The group's recording of the song "We Are the World" (as well as its later album of the same name)[4] benefited victims of a devastating famine in Ethiopia. Moreover, Springsteen had joined Amnesty International's Human Rights Now! tour in the fall of 1988. More recently, in March 1995, his song "Streets of Philadelphia" from the film *Philadelphia* won an Academy Award as best film song of 1994.[5] The song is narrated from the perspective of the film's main character: a promising, young, gay Philadelphia lawyer who contracts HIV/AIDS.

With this song, Springsteen widened his arc of concern to include the often-marginalized gay community. With "The Ghost of Tom Joad" and the other songs he was writing at this time, that arc would continue to widen: he would tell the stories of other men and women whom society's callousness and selfishness had sought to render invisible and unheard.

Within these tales of human deprivation, Springsteen said later, "the precision of the storytelling" would become "very important." "When you get the music and lyrics right in these songs," he continued, "your voice disappears into the voices of those you've chosen to write about."[6] Now he would attempt to provide a voice to some of these voiceless folk.

In "The Ghost of Tom Joad" Springsteen sought to introduce to a new generation the characters about whom Steinbeck had written so intensely in the late 1930s. This was no exercise in historical nostalgia, but rather a living challenge issued to the people and powers of his own day. In his opening lines Springsteen describes the daily reality of those who crowd the highways west in search of jobs and justice: police surveillance, homelessness, insecurity. "Welcome to the new world order," he sings sarcastically as he looks out upon this threadbare existence and threadbare hope—an ironic reference to the elder President Bush's use of that phrase in his claims of victory in the Cold War and the Persian Gulf.

Springsteen is emphasizing that we are not just talking about the Great Depression here. The deprivation and hopelessness of which Steinbeck wrote, and of which he, Springsteen, now sings, is *still* the reality for too many people in our land. Like so many of his generation, Tom Joad may be long gone, but his "ghost"—the challenge he presents, the stark and bitter reality he exposes—remains as much a part of American life as ever.

This is not necessarily the way we might like to view ourselves as a nation. American popular culture may offer exalted visions of the "American dream," and our leaders may speak of how, for the average American, things are getting better all the time. Many may buy into such national myths of superiority and progress. But others aren't fooled. Life may be hard, and the road may be long, but "nobody's kiddin' nobody" about it leading to any greener pastures or land of milk and honey, just as for so many of Steinbeck's Okies the arduous trek to California led only to new deprivation and even greater poverty. For so many poor and disenfranchised in America in our own day, the future seems to offer merely continued homelessness, hunger, and violence.

It is in how we meet the unmet needs of these downtrodden men and women that we will be judged. In the spirit of the Gospel of Matthew, Springsteen reminds us that it is in assisting these, the least of our brothers and sisters, that we truly honor the God who is within us (Matt. 25:40). To prove our worth—as individuals and as a nation—we, like Joad, must declare our oneness with the dispossessed, from the youngest to the oldest, with all those "strugglin' to be free."

Like the preacher who lives in a cardboard box beneath the underpass, we too wait for that promised time when the last shall be first and the first shall be last, when in the words of Mary's Magnificat (Luke 1:46–55) the lowly shall be exalted and the hungry shall be filled with good things. But while the "arc of the moral universe . . . bends toward justice, " as the great Unitarian preacher Theodore Parker intoned, Martin Luther King's quoting Parker's words a century later also reminds us that that arc is long. There is, in the ways of human affairs, no inevitable moral or ethical progress onward and upward forever.

Sometimes our society defaults on the debts it owes to those through whose labor its wealth has been achieved. In the song "Youngstown," Springsteen traces the history of that northeastern Ohio city, both to portray the development of the American industrial powerhouse and to trace the breakdown of the American social contract. In 1803, Springsteen sings, two brothers named James and Danny Heaton discovered iron ore in Yellow Creek and soon built a blast furnace for smelting iron. The area was an important arms manufacturer during the Civil War, and shortly thereafter a burgeoning steel industry led to economic prosperity and plenty of jobs for everyone, and Youngstown became a magnet for many of those in search of the American Dream.

It was no paradise, certainly. The work was hard, the furnaces were "hotter than hell," and "soot and clay" belched from tall smokestacks, soiling the environment and darkening the sky. But it gave people good work to do and provided a sense of purpose to their existence. There was a spirit of community and continuity, as one generation followed another into the steel mills.

But while the American dream might promise that such hard work and dedication will be rewarded with the blessings of prosperity, such is not always the case. Even though the workers of Youngstown (and countless industrial cities across our land) kept their side of the bargain—they labored hard, defended the nation in wars overseas, and sent their children to war as well—the other side ("them big boys" who own the mills and make the economic decisions that affect everyone) didn't. In order to maximize profits for themselves, they pulled out, closed down the mills, and sent the work off elsewhere. In their wake, they created a devastated social and economic landscape and engendered a deep sense of betrayal—a living hell of disappointment and despair—among those left behind to fend for themselves.

You Know the Rest

A good society will help people to do good: to exercise positive options; treat others decently; live lives that strive to meet something of their deeper potential. It is nonsense to think that people will make good choices all the time and will never give in to their base or selfish instincts. But perhaps societies can at least reward those who do what they're supposed to and play by the rules.

The narrator of the song "Straight Time" seems to want to live a life on the right side of the law. One of the first things he does when he gets out of prison is get married. He hopes that this domestication of his previously wild ways will help him stay out of jail, and maybe even save his life.

But the only work an ex-con like him can find is just awful: at a rendering factory, a slaughterhouse, amid the death and decay of rotting animal carcasses. "It ain't gonna make me rich," the ex-con sings in a masterpiece of understatement. It's not going to give him much of a sense of purpose in his life or reason to get up in the morning either.

As another of his weary days drags on and he is faced with the meaninglessness and sheer drudgery of his law-abiding existence, he considers the other possibilities open to him. His thoughts soon revert to the only other "trade" he knows: that of a common criminal. He doesn't want to go back to prison; he's "sick of doin' straight time" there, he sings. But he also looks at the probable trajectory of his life outside of prison and realizes that it, too, offers little more than an uninterrupted, dreary pathway direct to the grave.

His life seems to have become a prison on whichever side of the bars he happens to reside. At supper one night, his uncle slips him a hundred-dollar bill for his help in the uncle's stolen car ring; a hundred dollars is probably substantially more than he would make for a full day's work at the rendering plant. As is often the case in this fallen world, evil pays much better than goodness, in the short run at least. While prison was at times dreadful, he reminds himself that a person can get used to anything. He did at least survive the ordeal, which might be more than he can say of his present cussed existence.

As the song ends, he seems set to give in to the temptation to rejoin the ranks of the criminal. He has sawed the barrel off his hunting rifle, readying the tool of his reclaimed trade. As he lies in bed at night, he can't get the smell from his hands. Whether it's the smell of rendering or the smell of crime, we don't know for sure. What is certain is that it is the odor of death: the odor of a life not worth living, a life that can claim no life-giving hope as its own.

As creatures with free choice, we are responsible for the choices we make—and if we make irresponsible choices, we will sooner or later reap the whirlwind. But a society that fails to honor its own social contract debases the choices that all people have to make. If society is rife with greed, selfishness, and narcissism, then there would seem very little possibility of ameliorating the tragic choices to which these sins can give rise.

"Highway 29" starts off promisingly enough with a rather charming flirtation ritual in a local shoestore. The salesman tells the woman he's waiting on that smoking is prohibited; they exchange a bit of conversation, then telephone numbers, and then he slips his hand "up her skirt"—and everything goes downhill quickly from there.

In a flash, the pair moves from conversing in a shoe store and courting in a roadhouse to robbing a bank. It was inevitable, the narrator seems to believe; perhaps he's been down this highway before. "Well, I had a gun," he sings. "You know the rest." The robbery is botched, shots are fired, there is blood all over the place, and perhaps even a dead body is left behind as the pair flees down Highway 29.

The woman is in tears as she ponders how saying yes to this loser has brought her to this terrifying place. The man contemplates what he knows must be his imminent demise. Finally—tragically, too late—he comes to some realization that he has only himself to blame for this mess (and all the others that have come before this one, no doubt). He wants to blame his newfound mate, or society, or the people who have all that he doesn't have for his failures. But as he drives, he realizes that the devil isn't outside the car, or even in the seat beside him, but deep inside himself. "I knew it was something in me," he sings, something that has been with him through most of his life. Now that brokenness in his soul has led him to this tragic end in a pile of wreckage along a Mexican highway. As death approches, the man receives perhaps the first beatific vision he has ever had; as he falls into that final sleep, for the only time in his life perhaps, he feels himself escape the bondage of his own inner demons.

A Price in Return

We were told in "The Ghost of Tom Joad" that "the highway is alive" with people searching for work. In several songs on this album there is a striking sense of movement, of dislocation, of people traveling long distances—from state to state, even crossing international boundaries—in search of better prospects for themselves and their families. But while (for some) this great migration might offer a somewhat better economic situation, there are always great risks. Often the end result is tragic and even ends in death; at other times the body survives but the soul is deeply maimed.

Frank had ridden the rails since the Great Depression, we are told in the opening lines of "The New Timer." For some folks, things haven't really gotten all that much better since then. The song's narrator, a much younger man, also leaves his home (in Pennsylvania) looking for work. He meets Frank in East Texas, and from there they continue to move further west. "From New Mexico to Colorado, California to the sea," the narrator sings, sounding just a little like the chorus from "This Land Is Your Land." His list of jobs is almost as varied as the locales where he has stayed: farming sugar beets, picking peaches, driving farm machinery on the Great Plains, working in a lumber yard. He says that this is work he does just until he can get back on his feet, but that day apparently never arrives. He has to keep on moving merely to survive, sometimes being treated no better than an animal in a barn.

But even survival isn't guaranteed, not even for a wise old hand like Frank. After a long absence, the song's narrator hears Frank call out his name as he rides by on a train car carrying grain. But then shortly thereafter Frank is found shot dead, a victim of random, meaningless violence—an event that seems to shake whatever confidence the narrator had in the meaning of it all.

Looking out at a seemingly happy family in their little house by the side of the railroad tracks, the narrator ponders all that his nomadic life has cost him, most especially the separation from his little son. This lifetime of losses has left a coldness inside of him. He "picks [his] campsite carefully" now, he says, lest he meet the same fate as his comrade Frank. He lies in bed with a machete close at hand and prays to Jesus to feel hope and faith and love again, but these graces never arrive. Instead, as he lies awake, he just stares out at a darkness beyond that matches the darkness that now exists within.

Many of the songs on *The Ghost of Tom Joad* take place in locales in the U.S. Southwest or in Mexico. In these works, Springsteen expresses his concern for the difficult situation faced by many immigrants (often illegals) coming to the United States looking for work and a better life. Here many face issues of racism and exclusion in addition to the usual challenges of poverty and powerlessness. Springsteen wrote of these characters that their skin was darker and their language was different from that of the people he had written of earlier in his career, but they were people "trapped by the same brutal circumstances."[7]

With an alarming degree of regularity in *The Ghost of Tom Joad*, these circumstances prove not only brutal but fatal as well. In "Balboa Park," Springsteen sings of the "border boys" who cross the border between Mexico and California and come to San Diego to sell their bodies to prosperous "men in their Mercedes." Exploited in every way imaginable, these young male prostitutes live (and often die) on the streets. They send home some of their earnings; the rest goes toward their own subsistence—and, very often, toward drugs (especially "toncho"—inhalants).

"Sinaloa Cowboys" tells the story of two brothers, Miguel and Louis Rosales, who also cross the border illegally into California. But unlike the "border boys" of "Balboa Park," the Rosales brothers try to make a living for themselves legally—at least at first. They put in long, backbreaking hours working in the fruit orchards of the San Joaquin Valley "doing the work the *hueros* [Anglos] wouldn't do."

They work hard but have very little to show for it. When word reaches them that some men are looking for workers in an illegal methamphetamine plant not far away, they jump at the opportunity. At first it seems to pay off: working just a couple of days cooking meth, they can earn the equivalent of a year's salary in the orchards. But there are costs, of course—extremely steep ones. As their father had reminded Miguel and Louis when they headed north, "For everything the north gives, it exacts a price in return."

Producing methamphetamine is extremely dangerous, and, tragically, Louis pays for their newfound prosperity with his life when the shack in which he is working explodes. With extremely touching imagery, Springsteen describes how Miguel lifts his brother's dead body into the back of their pickup, drives all night to a eucalyptus grove, then buries Louis in the same hole where they had stored all their savings—ten thousand dollars.

It must have seemed like a princely sum to them at one time. Objectively, of course, it seems like a pittance balanced against what it has cost them in the end. But the story of Louis and Miguel is not all that unusual, and Springsteen is reminding us here that the poor always pay full price. Those without power and influence never come out ahead. They always pay disproportionately with their lives, whether in war or in peacetime. No one can put a value on a human life, least of all Miguel, who loved his brother dearly.

But given the intrinsic unfairness of the world, it might, sadly, have seemed like the best deal the Rosales brothers could hope for.

The Choices We Make

As we have seen, the works of Bruce Springsteen in general and *The Ghost of Tom Joad* in particular are strewn with the broken lives of people who have made absolutely awful decisions. But even within the Springsteen worldview, people aren't bound to choose poorly. Sometimes people are motivated by something more than their own particular needs and wants, or their accumulated anger, or their own limiting prejudices. Sometimes they actually manage to transcend these barriers and act out of compassion for another or in accord with the common good.

Carl, the narrator of "The Line," seems like a rather unremarkable figure. He describes himself as being "good at doin' what I was told," and his life story up to this point would seem to bear him out. Having been discharged from the army, Carl takes a job as a border guard. His wife dies, and he senses that his life is in flux and that there is an emptiness inside him yearning to be filled.

Soon Carl becomes friends with Bobby Ramirez, an American of Mexican lineage who has been a border guard for ten years. Because Bobby has relatives still living in Mexico, being a border guard is for him more than just a job. He senses the futility of the work the Border Patrol is doing: rounding up those who try to sneak across the border and sending them back home to Mexico, only to have them turn around and attempt the same dangerous endeavor once again. "Carl, hunger is a powerful thing," Bobby tells his friend.

As it is for the body, so too for the soul. From the moment Carl sets his eyes upon Luisa, a lovely dark-haired Mexican woman, his guarded and well-controlled approach to life falls away. When he sees her with a child in her arms as she waits in a holding pen with others who have been caught trying to cross the border illegally, he immediately offers his assistance. As he looks into Luisa's eyes, he is reminded of the loss of his wife the year before—something, no doubt, he has been keeping as far from his tough outer façade as possible. Soon Carl is fraternizing with Luisa at a bar in Tijuana. She tells him her life story, they dance, and, almost immediately it seems, Carl is in on their plan to slip her, her child, and her younger brother into the United States.

On the chosen night, the illegal immigrants climb into Carl's pickup, and the four of them head toward the American side of the border. But as they drive, Carl spies the tape across Luisa's brother's chest: he realizes that he has been betrayed. Ramirez rushes to intercept them before they reach the highway, and he and Carl face off against each other in the glare of their trucks' headlights. Carl feels his gun in his pocket but doesn't draw it. Ramirez considers reporting Carl's malfeasance to his superiors, but he ends up not saying anything to anyone about the incident. Luisa, her baby clutched in her arms, runs "off through the arroyo," presumably to a new life in the United States

Carl resigns from the Border Patrol six months later. The outer scope of his life resumes the same sad emptiness it had had before: he is alone once more, his work holds no adventure or meaning for him, and he searches the local bars, hoping to spy his Luisa once again.

But however mired in sadness Carl's life still is, he has emerged from his experience on the border a changed man. For once in his life, at least, he broke out of the straightjacket of self-control and followed the dictates of his heart. He even risked everything (his job, his reputation, his freedom, perhaps even his life) to meet the deeper aspirations of another human soul. Unfortunately, this sacrifice guaranteed him nothing of personal happiness or worldly fulfillment. But in that experience, at least, Carl transcended the ranks of the mundane and joined, if only for the briefest while, the order of the heroic.

At other times we make the decent choice only reluctantly, only after a long and tortuous ordeal in which our deepest values are called into question. The song "Galveston Bay" tells of Le Bing Son, a Vietnamese émigré who comes to America (a "promised land" as he sees it) and settles in a small town along the Gulf Coast of Texas. Le works hard as a machinist, saves his money, and, like many of his fellow refugees, buys a boat and harvests shrimp in the waters of Galveston Bay.

The other major character in "Galveston Bay" is Billy Sutter, an American veteran of the Vietnam War, who also works as a shrimper off the Texas coast. As more and more refugees settle in their area—and fish the same waters they do—Billy and other native-born Americans grow increasingly resentful. "America for Americans" becomes their rallying cry, and soon the Texas chapter of the Ku Klux Klan enters the fray, fanning racist emotions.

A plot to burn the boats owned by the Vietnamese is hatched. But soon after the fires are lighted, Le Bing Son shoots and kills two of the arsonists. He is tried for murder but is acquitted after pleading self-defense, a verdict that angers Billy and his white cohorts. As Le leaves the courthouse, Billy vows to him, "My friend, you're a dead man."

On his chosen night of revenge, Billy waits, hidden in the shadows on the docks. He has a knife, which he intends to use on Le. He watches as Le passes in front of him and stops to light a cigarette. The perfect opportunity for vengeance is at hand. But instead of striking, Billy puts the knife back into his pocket, and Le walks away.

Early the next morning, Billy resumes his normal life: as his wife sleeps, he kisses her softly and heads off to his boat. The same prejudices perhaps remain within him. His anger and fear perhaps remain unexorcised. In many ways, perhaps, he remains unchanged from the experience of the night before. But in other ways, of course, that night represented an epic moment for him: in that instant, standing in the shadows, with the vulnerable Le before him, he turned away from doing evil. Whatever his residual feelings about the Vietnamese (and about all those different from him and his tribe), Billy had been recruited for the forces of malevolence but had refused to join. In so doing, he created a fragile bridgehead of goodness there on Galveston Bay.

What Are We without Hope in Our Hearts?

Memory is often bitter, but it can be blessed as well. Even bitter memories move us forward; they are part of the experience of life that brings us to the present moment. In the living present, hope can flower and new possibilities (however bitter the past realities were) can be born.

As lightning flashes on the horizon and the heat and dryness of the desert surround him, the narrator of "Dry Lightning" has a vision of his lost lover. It is an almost enchanted specter of a "beautiful spirit" descended to earth on a vigorous Appaloosa—far different from her more tawdry reality as a dancer (perhaps even a prostitute) in that Monterey strip club where he first met her. But he has been so enchanted by her—by "the heat of her blood" and the "sweet smell of her skin"—that even though their relationship is dead and gone, memories of her linger. His mythologized vision of her seems to battle in his memory with more realistic remembrances of their fights and how unfulfilling their relationship actually was. Their passion was, no doubt, not unlike the dry lightning that now threatens off on the horizon: all fire but no relief, destined ultimately to burn unabated, perhaps inflicting no little damage in its wake. But it was dramatic, and it has carved its place deep in his memory.

On the other hand, the beatific vision offered in "Across the Border" is unequivocally glowing. The geographic "border" here refers to that between the United States and Mexico, but its connotation is much broader. The tonight/tomorrow dichotomy presented in the opening lines presents a clear psychological demarcation. "Tonight my bag is packed," the narrator sings. Tomorrow I will be "across the border" at last. Tomorrow my lover and I will be reunited; we will sleep beneath the open sky in each other's arms. Tomorrow, when that border is crossed, everything will change: pain and sadness will be banished, and we will drink at last the water of life. Life on one side of the line will be fundamentally different from that on the other.

In addition to the psychological dimension, the border that is being crossed may well be that most fundamental boundary of all: that between life and death. The images of the "other side" Springsteen presents here are too resplendent to refer to any merely earthly locale; everything is just too perfect. There is almost unimaginable abundance, with the perfume of flowers sweetening the air and the entire landscape swathed in "gold and green," and cascading mountain streams irrigating fertile plains. Indeed, this new land is a place where "pain and memory have been stilled"; it is clearly no place that exists in the earthly experience of any of us, however comfortable our surroundings or uncomplicated our lives.

Only in heaven has memory been stilled, and pain is no more. Only in heaven do past, present, and future blend in the blessedness of eternity's sunrise.

Perhaps the narrator's beloved (he calls her his *corazon*, his very heart) has already passed on across that eternal border. Now he sings of her, and dreams of her, and pledges that he will remain strong, even in the face of losing her. Then, with the hope in his heart that they will meet again, he invokes "the saints' blessing and grace" as he both prepares to bid her farewell and prepares for his own journey to that blessed place where they will meet again.

In this greater realm of God's justice, their ultimate hopes will be realized. Here, all will be offered a cup from "God's blessed waters" (rather than the "muddy waters" a more earthly stream like the Rio Bravo offers). Here, in the reign of divine justice, there will be no more divisions between "haves" and "have-nots," between those who belong and those who don't. Rather, at last, all will share in the abundance of love and fortune poured forth, like a mighty stream, across the face of all existence.

Chapter Ten

From Good Friday to Easter

The Rising

On December 8, 1998, Jon Landau Management issued a press release, the opening paragraph of which read simply, "Jon Landau Management has confirmed that Bruce Springsteen intends to begin a worldwide tour with the E Street Band in the summer of 1999." Additional details would be forthcoming after the first of the year, the announcement concluded.[1] Springsteen had officially disbanded the E Street Band in October 1989, although they had played together a few times since then. Now, much to the delight of fans worldwide, Bruce Springsteen and the E Street Band were to be reunited once again.

On March 15, 1999, they played four songs as Bruce was inducted into the Rock and Roll Hall of Fame in Cleveland. The very next month, the Reunion Tour began with a series of shows in Barcelona, Spain. After two months of critically acclaimed shows across Europe, the band came home to the United States.

A monumental reception awaited them: fifteen shows at the Continental Airlines Arena in New Jersey were sold out as soon as they were put on sale.[2] By the time the tour reached its thunderous conclusion at Madison Square Garden in New York City a full year later, the Reunion Tour was an unmitigated triumph. Altogether the band had been on the road fifteen months and played 133 shows, most of them completely sold out, in 62 different cities. Chris Willman of *Entertainment Weekly* said that the tour "was as much traveling tent revival as reunion tour."[3]

Writing in *Z Magazine,* Sandy Carter said, "As we come to the end of the 20th century, it's increasingly difficult to believe in the power of rock and roll to change lives. But with the current reunion tour of Bruce Springsteen and the E Street Band, the tradition rediscovers a glorious, life-affirming eloquence."[4]

The tour was not without controversy. Springsteen's debut of a new song, "American Skin (41 Shots)" on June 4, 2000, at the Phelps Arena in Atlanta, called the wrath of the New York City Police Department down upon his head. The song dealt with the case of Amadou Diallo, a West African immigrant killed outside his Bronx apartment house in February 1999. Policemen looking for a rape suspect fired forty-one rounds at Diallo, who was killed instantly. They thought he was reaching for a gun. It turned out Diallo was unarmed; perhaps he was trying to get his wallet to confirm his identity.

The reaction in official police circles to "American Skin" was immediate: The president of New York's Policemen's Benevolent Association urged a boycott of Springsteen's concerts. Bob Lucente, president of the New York State Fraternal Order of Police unleashed a tirade in front of news microphones, labeling Bruce a "fucking dirtbag" and "a floating fag."[5] Lucente soon was forced to issue an apology to gay police officers offended at his remarks, and within a few weeks he had been replaced as F.O.P. president.

Springsteen hadn't intended "American Skin" as an attack on the police or even as a mere screed against police brutality or racial profiling. Rather, he was pushing all Americans toward a thorough examination of racism in all its forms in our society. "I was asking some questions that are hanging very heavy in the air right now," he told an interviewer. "We have a very large part of the population, people of color in the United States, who are viewed through a veil of criminality, who have been used to having their full citizenship denied. . . . It's one of the issues America is going to have to face."[6]

But in spite of the "American Skin" controversy, the Reunion Tour headed toward a climactic conclusion at Madison Square Garden on July 1. The buoyant, optimistic spirit generated by the reunited band was captured best, perhaps, in the song with which Bruce had chosen to close almost every one of the tour's shows.

"Land of Hope and Dreams" was one of the few new songs debuted during the reunion. The song seemed deeply influenced both by the popular gospel hymn "This Train Is Bound for Glory" as well as by "People Get Ready" by the great African American composer and performer Curtis Mayfield.

Unlike the train featured in the gospel song, that in "Land of Hope and Dreams" welcomes *everyone* onboard. The traditional version demanded that its riders be "righteous"; there was no room for sinners here. "This train don't carry gamblers, no pickpockets nor hobo ramblers," its lyrics declared. Springsteen's train, on the other hand, "carries saints and sinners . . . losers and winners." Even "whores and gamblers" are explicitly welcome in its boarding party, as are all "lost souls."

The honored and despised, the foolish and the wise—all people are welcome on board this train as it proceeds on its journey. All people are needed to complete the full panorama of human be-ing. All must be saved if there is to be any hope for any of us. And all shall be saved if we hold steadfast to our faith in the ability of men and women to take care of one another, stand by one another, and help one another to heal; if we remain committed to our hope and our vision of the more glorious land that can be. We may never see this land of hope and dreams with human eyes within this lifetime. But we know that it truly abides, as an almost heavenly vision, out on the horizon's edge. It is toward that vision—toward realization of these deeper hopes and dreams—that all our actions in this world must be pointed.

September 11

Springsteen had retired to his New Jersey estate at the conclusion of the Reunion Tour, to begin writing songs for a new album. Buoyed by the reception the tour had engendered, and inspired by the ability of the E Streeters to make great music after their prolonged separation, he was determined that it would be a full-band, full-throttle rock and roll effort, bringing him and the band back to their more carefree, spontaneous roots.

Then came the attacks of September 11, 2001. On that morning, Springsteen later told a reporter from *Time* magazine, "I was having breakfast, and then I was in front of the television set. . . . I drove across the local bridge. The Trade Center sits right in the middle of it when you look toward New York."[7] The Twin Towers were now gone, the sky was empty and the world was changed.

Shortly after the attacks, Springsteen was driving near his home. As he pulled out of the parking lot at nearby Sea Bright beach, the driver of a passing car rolled down his window and shouted at him, "We need you—*now!*"[8] The New Jersey county where Springsteen lived, Monmouth, had lost 158 people in the World Trade Center attack—more than any other county in the state. His neighbors were in mourning. Springsteen discovered that many people were looking to him to help them find some meaning amid the tragedy. Within days of September 11, Springsteen was responding to the calamity by writing songs.[9]

A national telethon to benefit the families of those killed in the attacks was scheduled for September 21. Springsteen opened the program, which was aired nationally by all major networks and broadcast in over two hundred countries worldwide. He had originally considered performing "Into the Fire," one of the new songs he had written, but ultimately decided on "My City of Ruins," a song he had written for his adopted hometown, Asbury Park, and which he had performed a few times there already. Later, in introducing "My City of Ruins" at other benefits, Springsteen would say, "This was a song that I wrote for Asbury Park. Songs go out into the world and hopefully they end up where people need 'em. So I guess this is a gift from Asbury Park to New York City in its time of need."[10]

Amid somber gospel strains, "My City of Ruins" describes a portrait of death, destruction, and despair. There's blood on the ground; a cold rain falls, and all is darkness. In the distance an organ sounds, but in an empty church. Church bells ring, but they are largely ignored. There are "young men on the corner like scattered leaves." A city (and, by extension, a nation) wanders aimlessly, trying to find some meaning amid the destruction. Once bustling, vibrant streets are devoid of people. Some fall to their knees in prayer. Across the face of the city, there is nothing but devastation.

But then, from deep within, as though from the very heart of the earth itself, a voice arises and calls out, "Come on, rise up! Come on, rise up!"

In Springsteen's words here, there is a clear echo of earlier words by Thomas Wolfe from his novel *You Can't Go Home Again:* "But under the pavements, trembling like a cry, under the waste of time, under the hoof of the beast above the broken bones of cities, there will be something growing like a flower, something bursting from the earth again, forever deathless, faithful, coming into life again like April."[11]

Even in the first hours of the city's destruction were planted the seeds of its resurrection.

It will be no easy resurrection, certainly. It will, at times, be a soul-wearying and heart-breaking one. It is not a city in abstract that lies dead or dying here; it is, in the case of the World Trade Center attacks, almost three thousand human souls who have been taken. For those left behind, there is that intimately personal void that will never be filled. So many thousands of survivors will despair that life can even continue at all after such a devastating loss. Tell me, how do I begin again? they will ask. Not just my physical surroundings, but my very life—my very reason for being alive—is now in ruins.

Resurrection is hard work. It requires full engagement of our human hands—in all the physical labor that needs to be performed, in reaching out to those who need healing, and, not the least, in prayer—seeking the courage, faith, and love needed to bind up the broken and raise up the devastated city once again. In "My City of Ruins," Springsteen suggests that we look within (and beyond) and seek to discern the divine light we will need to find our way through this encircling gloom.

The voice persists. "Come on, rise up!" Springsteen sings over and over again, imploring those around him not to quit. Imploring our nation not to quit. Imploring people of goodwill everywhere not to quit. Not least of all, imploring himself to keep on with the struggle.

Springsteen implores us to rise up and not to stop until the city is rebuilt, the nation is healed, and the lives of those who have been taken are redeemed.

Art Responds to Life

By the beginning of 2002, Bruce felt he had enough decent material to head into the studio and make a record. Searching for a solid, unambiguous rock sound this time around, he sought out a new producer. He found one of the foremost in the business: Brendan O'Brien, who had worked previously with a host of contemporary rock and roll's leading acts, including Pearl Jam, Aerosmith, Limp Bizkit, Red Hot Chili Peppers, and Rage Against the Machine. By February, Bruce and the band were recording with O'Brien at Southern Tracks studio in Atlanta. By the end of June, work on the album—titled *The Rising*—was completed.

Never before had a work by Springsteen been so eagerly anticipated. Even before its release, *The Rising* was being heralded in the mainstream media as the first major cultural response to the events of September 11. Springsteen, so often in the past private to the point of being a recluse, was all over the airwaves. On the day *The Rising* was released, July 30, 2002, NBC's *Today Show* dedicated an entire program, two full hours, to Springsteen and his new album. The E Street Band appeared on *Late Night with David Letterman* on two successive nights. Ted Koppel interviewed Springsteen on *Nightline* for three straight evenings. A large segment of America, it seemed, was looking to Bruce Springsteen to sum up the national experience of 9/11.

However excessive the hype became at times, and as impossible as it would be for any single work to become the definitive cultural expression of the September 11 attacks, *The Rising* emerged as an almost epic reflection of those sad events. The stories, emotions, and impressions of September 11 seem to breathe from just about every song.

From the very first number, "Lonesome Day," it is as though Springsteen is taking us all by the hand again, not "to case the promised land" this time, but to lead us back to that saddest day of all.

As "Lonesome Day" begins, the singer ponders how he really didn't know the person he thought he knew. Early impressions of a "sweet whisper" and a "tender touch" quickly degenerate in the second verse into a changed reality of a "dark sun" rising, storms passing through; a house burning, and a viper lying in the grass. The narrator longs for revenge, but then ultimately chooses acquiescence. "This too shall pass," he prays. Somehow, he knows— though he's probably not sure how—he'll make it through "this lonesome day."

One could, of course, read this song from a much narrower lens than that provided by September 11: as simply the aftermath of the (perhaps sudden and unexpected) ending of a relationship. Indeed, many (maybe even most) of the songs on *The Rising* can be read either as September 11-inspired or as more universal meditations on the blessings and curses of human life. But as much can be said about decent poetry in general. Good poems often have particular reference points (they refer to some particular events in the lives of the characters involved), but they also resonate within us in some more general, even universal, way. Part of Springsteen's continuing genius is that one may choose to listen either in the personal or the universal key without undermining the integrity of the other. "Lonesome Day" and other songs on *The Rising* work as ruminations on the events of September 11, 2001, but they also work as more general meditations on our human condition.

Someplace Higher

The first draft of the song "Into the Fire" was written only a few days after September 11. As such, it represents Springsteen's most immediate and direct response to this great tragedy. "The sky was falling and streaked with blood," the song begins, and the narrator watches as the firefighter whom she (or he) loves disappears into the doomed towers, "into the dust," then "up the stairs, into the fire."

At such times of duty, true public servants cannot cling to personal needs and wants. They must leave behind those who depend on them most intimately in order to serve the common good. They must let loose the hands of those closest to them in order to serve the general welfare, their true business. In spite of the entreaties of those left behind at home, a higher calling lifts them to go where they are most needed. Sometimes—especially at times of crisis such as September 11—they pay for their response with their very lives. The New York City Fire Department lost 343 firefighters in the 9/11 attack. "Into the Fire" is Springsteen's tribute to them and to all who die in the line of duty.

According to Springsteen's own interpretation of the song, "Into the Fire" begins as blues and ends as gospel.[12] Once the sad reality of sacrifice is mourned, Springsteen's verses explode into the living gospel of lives well lived. From the examples of those who have perished, Springsteen chants, may we seek and find the spirit we need—the faith, hope, and love we need—to go on with our lives and transcend this tragedy. "May your faith give us faith, may your hope give us hope," he sings again and again. It is through our human care for one another—our heroism, our sacrifice, our love—that we can raise one another to our full humanity.

Of all the songs on *The Rising*, "Into the Fire" is the one most literally bound to the events of September 11. But even here there are more general reference points. This song's invocation of deeper powers to *uplift* us is hardly unique in the Springsteen worldview. Most notably, perhaps, in "Badlands" on *Darkness on the Edge of Town,* there was also a summoning forth of "the love that you gave me, the faith that can save me," as well as a hope and a prayer that we might be *raised* above our present, wretched state. These deeper powers might come from within ourselves, or from a higher source, or from the genuine interaction of human souls. The exact locus of this something greater will differ for each of us, but what is important in Springsteen's view is that there is this "something more" that can be called upon to get us through our times of deepest distress.

Heaven in My Heart

When the easy optimism of "Waitin' on a Sunny Day" passes (the song was written in 1999, so it serves, perhaps, as a good enough reflection of that somehow "simpler" world before September 11, 2001), we come face to face with the realism and even despair of "Nothing Man," a sad, mournful tune about a man whose life has been rendered empty and void by some terrible ordeal he has endured.

Interestingly, "Nothing Man" is perhaps the oldest song on *The Rising*. It was originally written in 1994 about a Vietnam veteran suffering from post-traumatic stress syndrome. The main character in "Nothing Man" has physically survived some great, traumatic event in his life but still feels a lingering, living death as a result of what he has been through.

The man has been lauded by his "hometown paper" for his tribulation; perhaps he's even been called a hero by the people around him, who want to buy him a drink and shake his hand. Everyone around him seems able to get on with life; they act "like nothing's changed." But even as he acknowledges the blessedness of the world outside of him (the blueness of the sky, for example), inside he feels nothing. He now perceives himself as "a nothing man," with no reason left to justify his remaining in this world. Now he lies in bed, contemplating the pistol ("the pearl and silver") on the night stand—and he prays for courage. We don't really know, of course, whether he's asking for the courage to pull the trigger or *not* to, whether he's reaching out for salvation or just escape.

With grace, or even sometimes simply with patience, our emptiness can be filled. Miracles of healing are not preordained, but they do occur. In "Countin' on a Miracle," Springsteen once again presents a portrait of the loss engendered by the events of September 11: "It's a fairytale so tragic," he sings, and nothing can "break the spell" of pain and loss. But as foolish as it might seem to others, the singer will cling to his hope for a "miracle"— his anticipation that things can turn out all right in the end. This is the best way he has available to him now to keep faith with the one stolen from him.

Of course, it's no "fairytale" at all that we're hearing about here; this survivor is not waiting for an easy miracle and a simple restoration of life as it was. He knows now that there will be no "happily ever after" ending to his tale. His love has been reduced to dust, quite literally, in the awful aftermath of the September 11 attacks. But out of the dust, the blessed strands of memory arise— the face, the ideals, the hopes, the dreams, the love he has known— and from these strands, he who is left behind is able to weave a pattern of life strong enough to allow him to go on.

There are no illusions here that life will ever be the same, or that life will be easy, or that loss is anything less than loss and pain anything less than pain. But life goes on. And even when they leave us, we have been blessed by the loves we have known; indeed, they form a heaven-like place in our hearts. Because of this gift of love we have received, we know that we have a debt to the future to keep the channels of love and life flowing.

Details of a Life, a Loss

September 11 was most poignantly, of course, a profound human tragedy, with so many thousands of lives shattered. It is in the simplest details of life that we are touched most deeply. We truly sense the havoc that this tragedy has wrought not in any philosophical or political or ideological manifestos, but in the simple loss of a single human life—a father or mother, a husband or wife, a lover, a son or daughter. If we multiply each of these individual human tragedies by close to three thousand, we can sense the true magnitude of this loss. Three thousand people might not seem like so many when we consider it in the context of the millions in New York City, or the hundreds of millions in the United States, or the billions in the world. They're just a few more raindrops in a seemingly endless sea.

But when we think of each individual human story—its power and grace, its spirit and history, the joy and tragedy that each manifests, that each life represents—then we realize how far and wide the arcs of sadness created by those three thousand raindrops in that once-calm sea truly are. Each being is a manifestation of an infinite power to touch and be touched, to love, to create. Each is a story all its own. Each is a precious human song, stilled too soon. So much power, strength, courage, love, faith, and hope reduced in a flash to dust and ashes.

Of all the songs on *The Rising*, perhaps it is "You're Missing" that provides the most precious, intimate portrait of this loss. In this song, Springsteen provides countless minute but significant details on one of these stolen lives. "Shirts in the closet, shoes in the hall," he begins, and he then proceeds to enumerate further examples of domestic routine: a visiting grandmother in the kitchen with the baby, a coffee cup sitting unmoved on the kitchen counter, a piece of clothing draped carelessly over the back of a chair. The morning newspaper has been delivered. Everything on the surface of things remains the same—but "you're missing," and so everything is changed.

That void which cannot be filled—that soul which cannot be replaced—creates other voids: there will be no answers to the entreaties of the children when they ask if everything will be all right; there will be no solace from (or for) those who call, wanting information or wanting to help; there will be no one with whom to share this house, this bed, this life. At least at first there will be no meaning to all of this, either. Even God is absent, off in a void somewhere. God is "drifting in heaven," and there is no knowing what evil the day's mail may bring. Where once there was a soul mate, there is now only the residue of dust in the air; where once there was joy, there is now nothing but tears.

The Days After

There are always the September 12ths of our lives, too—the mornings after tragedies, or great changes, or disruptions of our well-honed schedules. These are the times when we awaken to a changed landscape, to a different skyline, sometimes to an entirely "Empty Sky."

The empty space on the skyline is matched by the "empty impression" in the bed where our mate used to lie. When we arise from that bed, we have a decision to make. As we face a future we never anticipated, we need to decide in which direction we will head now: toward good or toward evil, down the road of love or the road of revenge. The desire for revenge ("an eye for an eye") may come quickly, even naturally, even understandably. But to honor that desire and not the more abiding force of love is to turn our back on our truer, more divine nature. It is to choose to cut our bow from the "tree of evil," and to usher in yet another cycle of violence, revenge, and recrimination.

There is a more excellent way, Springsteen—like Saint Paul in 1 Corinthians 12:31—reminds us. "There's a lot of walls need tearin' down," he sings in the breathlessly shallow "Let's Be Friends." It is up to each of us to "take them down one by one." In the boldly experimental song, "Worlds Apart," heavily influenced by the music of the Sufis, Springsteen sings about a love affair between a Muslim from the Middle East and a Westerner.[13]

No matter how great the obstacles and how dangerous the peril they face, this man and woman have chosen to love. Theirs is a choice between honoring the spirit of the living, or being devoured by the specters of the dead. In their loving, these two cry out to the whole world at this dangerous time in its history. As they plan to meet "on the ridge between these worlds apart," they are calling out to all people, East and West, to join them there.

Likewise in the song "Paradise," Springsteen speaks of the choices we all make between life and death, good and evil, embracing life or strangling it instead.

"Paradise" begins in the most harrowing manner, with the words of a suicide bomber as she replaces the schoolbooks in a backpack with plastic explosives and the wires of a homemade bomb. She then wanders into a marketplace to do her dastardly work. She holds her breath, closes her eyes, presumably sets off the bomb—"And I wait for paradise," she concludes.

Then, in the second verse, the scene shifts; we are back in the United States, in Virginia. The protagonist is a widow, a woman who lost her husband in the attack on the Pentagon. There is here, too, a yearning for paradise—for heaven—to see those we love once again.

Paradise doesn't come through the plotting of evil, of course. There is no heaven awaiting the one who takes innocent lives. Nor is it possible to see again, in this life, those who are now gone from us. In the final verse of "Paradise," the survivor in Virginia wades into a river and is completely submerged. Perhaps Springsteen is describing a suicide attempt here, or perhaps his words represent a metaphorical wading into the river that separates life from death.[14] In either case, the survivor knows that she can't remain underwater any longer and eventually comes to the surface once again. In the end, she realizes that she cannot rejoin her lost beloved in heaven somewhere. She can't relive those times that are now gone. Instead, she chooses to go on living—right now, in the living present. When she feels the warmth of the sun on her face, she understands that whatever paradise we will find, at least on this side of the river, comes to us through *living* each sacred, holy, breathing moment we have before us. In so doing, she affirms the words of the Sufi mystic Kabir: "Friend, do not wait for death to find heaven," Kabir said. "If you do not untie the knots that bind you now, do you expect the ghosts to do it after you die?" The blessed moment of being alive is what is truly holy.

The Power of Community

So much of Springsteen's work—as well as so much of truly mature and integrated religion—can be characterized as *defiantly hopeful*. Life is resplendent with hope in spite of all the tragic and mad and terrible things this world can do. This hope comes most fully to flower through our relationships with others.

The most upbeat song on *The Rising* is "Mary's Place." It may well be also the most explicitly religious. The lyrics share a chorus with the song "Meet Me at Mary's Place" by the great soul singer Sam Cooke, but there the lyrical similarities (and certainly the connotations of meaning) pretty much end.

It is not stretching things too far to intimate that "Mary's Place" is addressed to the Virgin Mary herself and not the Mary of "Thunder Road" and some of Springsteen's earlier works, or to some generic character who just happens to be named Mary. "I'm sure it's the Catholic coming out in me," Springsteen told Adam Sweeting from *Uncut* magazine. "[Mary] was always the most beautiful name."[15]

In "Mary's Place" Springsteen provides further evidence of his long, sometimes difficult effort to make peace with the Catholic faith into which he was born. Even if he isn't exactly singing an Exultet to the Blessed Virgin in this song, "Mary's Place" can be heard as an ode to that great figure of maternal comfort and grace and as a recognition of the need we all have for a community of faith to get us through the hard times of life.

Like so many people in the days following September 11, Springsteen found himself bringing his family back to church. This yearning for the power of community in times of need permeates "Mary's Place." Right from the start, of course, we know this will be no sentimental or sanctimonious "Ave Maria." Bruce's worldview is much too universalized for that: He's got "seven pictures of Buddha," he sings, and "the Prophet's on his tongue." There are also "eleven angels of mercy" mourning the havoc that has been wrought out on the horizon. Then there is the call of faith: "My heart's dark but it's rising." The singer is sad, but he yearns for hope; he summons forth the faith that is within him; he hears the blessed voice calling out to him—commanding him, really—to "meet me at Mary's Place," where "we're gonna have a party," where the celebration of life, the celebration of being joined in one community, will take place.

Here at last, in this blessed community of memory and hope, we'll get "this thing started." By "this thing," Springsteen could well infer a true spiritual revival that will transform the face of the world in an image of love and justice. "Mary's Place" sings forth the importance of communal celebration—and by extension religious worship—as the catalyst for ushering in a revolution in the sphere of human consciousness.

"Your loving grace surrounds me," Springsteen sings (such would be, of course, fine words for a good Catholic boy to address to the Mother of God). Surrounding the worshiper, too, is the loving grace of the community. James Joyce is supposed to have said that Catholicism means "Here comes everybody!" The church, for all its faults, is like a great big party, to which all people are welcome. It represents, within Christianity, a universal celebration of the entire body of Christ (and, by extension, the entire body of humanity), where we lose our small selves in the assembled crowd and feel ourselves held aloft, as though by heavenly arms.

In the midst of this reverie—this excitement of the community getting ready to be together—Springsteen pauses, like one who has just remembered in the midst of bliss a deep sadness, and asks, in words that could be addressed to Our Lady of Sorrows herself, "How do you live brokenhearted?" How do you go on living when that which you love has been taken from you?

Then he answers his own question: he remembers the picture in the locket he wears around his neck. It may be a picture of Mary; it may be a picture of the one he has lost. Either way, it is a constant reminder to him that love survives. "Blow on the coal of the heart," J. B.'s wife tells that modern Job at the end of the play by Archibald MacLeish. "Blow on the coal of the heart." That glow will light our way through the darkness that sadness brings.

How do we live brokenhearted? By lighting candles in the window, shining out at the whole world: "seven candles" in particular, the song says; one for each night and one for each day of the week, each day of creation. Light one candle each night "like the steadfast star," Emma Lazarus wrote in her poem about Hanukkah. "And add each night a lustre till afar" a Godlike splendor shines over all the earth. Pope John XXIII once referred to the seven cardinal virtues as the "seven candles of faith." Seven candles are often lit in the Catholic and Orthodox traditions to represent the seven sacraments.

"How do we get this thing started?" Springsteen then asks again. How do we overcome the tragedy of our times? By accepting the rain that falls upon us as part of the price we pay for being alive. By listening deeply for the song of life. By dropping to our knees and praying for divine guidance. By joining in the "shout from the crowd"—the Great Amen of the whole people of God. By turning up the volume of our religious imaginations and spiritual sensibilities. By not retreating into our pain but by joining with men and women of goodwill to remake the skylines of our world. "Mary's Place" is a song of spiritual celebration—celebration that can only be realized *in community*.

Life in the Midst of Death

Similarly the "li, li, li's" of the chorus of Springsteen's song "The Rising" can be heard as abbreviated alleluias—a song of life in the midst of death. "The Rising" is truly an Easterlike anthem arising out of the darkness and despair of September 11, a national Good Friday experience if there ever was one.

"The Rising" is narrated from the viewpoint of a New York City firefighter, racing into the flaming inferno of the World Trade Center.[16] This will be no easy journey, certainly, and soon we are taken right into the heart of the terror. "There's spirits above and behind me," Springsteen sings, meaning perhaps the ghosts of those who have already perished or those who are about to. The narrator's fellow firefighters seem almost haunted: their faces are dirty with grime and soot or have completely disappeared in the deep darkness; their eyes burn bright, with fear perhaps or simply reflecting the inferno that burns all around them. "May their precious blood bind me," Springsteen's firefighter prays as he stands before his own final judgment, invoking a prominent Catholic image of the blood of Christ.

The "li, li, li's" that then follow are the alleluias of a funeral mass, our prayers for the souls of our dearly departed brothers and sisters that usher them from this life to the next. Then comes the vision of transcendence and resurrection: The narrator sees Mary in the garden "of the thousand sighs" of Shakespeare's *Twelfth Night,* that is, a cemetery, where she weeps for the deceased, or comforts those who come to visit them there. Also in this beatific vision are "holy pictures of our children," and one is reminded of the portraits of those who were missing that were posted all around New York City in the days after September 11 like prayer cards of now departed saints.

These dear souls, these "children"—children of God, brothers and sisters of us all—are now "dancing in a sky filled with light." Their spirits have ascended; they are now one with God.

The narrator feels arms wrapped around him: they could be his memory of being held by the one he loved, or they could be the arms of the Almighty swooping him into the divine bosom; it is the same love that holds him close, either way. He feels his blood mixing in communion with all life. Then a blessed "dream of life" arrives, as vital and exuberant as a freshly caught catfish struggling to be loose of the fishing line, as vigorous and undying as a life that changes form perhaps, but truly has no end.

This "dream of life" pervades the remainder of the song. It becomes the refrain—the refutation of every challenge offered against life and the affirmation of everything worthy of praise within life. All darkness and sorrow, all tears and sadness, all fear and shadows are cast away in the light of this eternal dream. In the glory of its light, all love and mercy and memory abide forever, triumphantly.

A "burnin' wind"—the Holy Spirit of a new Pentecost—sweeps down, transforming our pain. And we are reminded, in this blessed life, that "neither death, nor life, nor angels, nor rulers, nor things present, nor things to come, nor powers, nor height, nor depth, nor anything else in all creation, will be able to separate us from the love of God" (Rom. 8:38–39).

We emerge from our experience in this world chastened and wounded, but *risen*—alive again. And in the breath of life, we sense the resilience of hope and the profound joy of human community upon this good earth.

Chapter Eleven

Citizen Springsteen
Devils & Dust

The success of *The Rising* established Bruce Springsteen as a sort of *eminence grise* of American rock and roll. Its corresponding tour was a commercial triumph: according to *Billboard,* the tour grossed nearly a quarter of a billion dollars over its two-year span, making it the highest-earning tour by any performer during that period.[1] The album had debuted at number one on the *Billboard* chart and eventually sold over three million units—by far Springsteen's best seller since *Tunnel of Love* rode the coattails of *Born in the U.S.A.* to triple platinum in 1987. When at the Grammy Awards in February 2003 Bruce and *The Rising* lost Album of the Year and Song of the Year honors to newcomer Norah Jones, the outcry from Springsteen fans (and much of the general public) was all but deafening. When asked by a reporter from *Entertainment Weekly* if Bruce had been "robbed" at the Grammys, Steven Van Zandt answered directly, "In a word, yeah."[2] But Springsteen soon got over whatever irritation he might have felt at being passed over in favor of Jones.[3] He opened the 2003 leg of the *Rising* tour five days later in Duluth, Minnesota. In March, the band headed to Australia and New Zealand for five shows; then, in the spring, it was back to North America, where most of April was spent traveling across Canada. A three-week break was then followed by another tour of Europe. By the summer of 2003, Springsteen and the band had begun the tour's final leg: a series of multinight stands in large stadiums across the continent, including famous baseball fields such as Fenway Park, Dodger Stadium, and Toronto's Skydome. Finally, the *Rising* tour came to a grand conclusion with a thirty-song megaconcert at Shea Stadium in New York on October 4, 2003, which even included a guest appearance by the legendary Bob Dylan during the encores.

But even after the tour was completed, Springsteen seldom left the public eye for long. He appeared with actor Michael J. Fox at a benefit for the Parkinson's Disease Foundation at the Stone Pony in Asbury Park on November 1. On November 11, *The Essential Bruce Springsteen* box set was released by Columbia, followed a week later by a new video, *Live in Barcelona.* Springsteen played three Christmas shows with the Max Weinberg 7 at the Convention Hall in Asbury Park in December; after a winter hiatus of several weeks, he traveled to Cleveland in March to help induct Jackson Browne into the Rock and Roll Hall of Fame. When his wife, Patti Scialfa, released a solo album in June 2004, however, Springsteen purposefully maintained a low profile in order not to steal attention from her.

On August 4, the Vote for Change Tour was announced: a wide array of rock artists, including Springsteen and the entire E Street Band, would participate in a series of concerts to benefit the anti-war group MoveOn.org and its political action committee (MoveOn PAC).[4] "We share a belief that this is the most important election of our lifetime," a joint declaration issued by the artists stated. "We are fighting for a government that is open, rational, just, and progressive. And we intend to be heard."[5] A series of concerts was scheduled for just before the election in closely contested states across the country.

Springsteen had become increasingly outspoken about his opposition to the war in Iraq, as well as his general antipathy toward the administration of President George W. Bush. Introducing "Born in the U.S.A." in Providence, Rhode Island, in March 2003—on the eve of the American invasion of Iraq—Springsteen couldn't have been more definite about where he stood: "I wrote this song in the early eighties about the Vietnam war," he said in Providence. "I wouldn't want to have to write another one like it.

I'll send this out tonight as a prayer for peace, a prayer for the safety of our sons and daughters, the safety of innocent Iraqi civilians, and to add our voices to no war in Iraq."[6] By the summer, Springsteen had added what he called a "public service announcement" to almost every concert—a two-minute monologue during which he stressed that the question of whether America had been misled into war wasn't "a liberal or conservative question," and that demanding truthfulness and accountability from our leaders was a responsibility for all citizens.[7]

Following the announcement of the Vote for Change Tour, however, Springsteen's pronouncements became more explicitly partisan. In "Chords for Change," an op-ed piece written for the *New York Times* on August 5, 2004, Springsteen recounted his frustration with the ability of those in power to tackle the severe questions America faced as a nation: "Why is it that the wealthiest nation in the world finds it so hard to keep its promise and faith with its weakest citizens?" he asked. "Why do we continue to find it so difficult to see beyond the veil of race? How do we conduct ourselves during difficult times without killing the things we hold dear? Why does the fulfillment of our promise as a people always seem to be just within grasp yet forever out of reach?"

The Democratic candidates for president and vice president, John Kerry and John Edwards, weren't perfect, Springsteen continued. But he did believe that they were "sincerely interested . . . in asking the right questions and working their way toward honest solutions." Then Springsteen offered a hint at a deeper impetus for openly taking sides in the election: "It is through the truthful exercising of the best of human qualities—respect for others, honesty about ourselves, faith in our ideals—that we come to life in God's eyes. It is how our soul, as a nation and as individuals, is revealed. . . . The country we carry in our hearts is waiting."[8]

Springsteen would repeat that phrase—"The country we carry in our hearts is waiting"—in introducing Kerry at a series of rallies in Ohio days before the election. Kerry's campaign had hoped that Springsteen's presence would rally uncommitted voters and push Ohio into the Democratic column. However, on Election Day, Ohio—and the nation—went for Bush.

Along with millions of other Americans, Springsteen was disappointed by the result. But neither exile nor hibernation was on his list of upcoming projects. Instead, after the election he went back into the studio with Brendan O'Brien, the producer with whom he had collaborated so successfully on *The Rising.* Within months, a new album was completed. A release date of April 26, 2005, was set for Springsteen's thirteenth opus (nineteenth if you counted various compilations), which would bear the title *Devils & Dust.*

What You Do to Survive

The album was a blend both of recently written songs along with some older, unreleased material. The oldest song on the record—"All the Way Home"—dated from 1991 and so was almost fourteen years old. The most recently composed song (dating from the spring of 2003) was the album's title track. The locus of the song, perhaps not surprising given what was going through Springsteen's mind at the time, was Iraq.

In "Devils & Dust," Springsteen sings from the perspective of an American solider trapped in a war far from home. This frightened, tired fighter takes his place in the line of literary veterans of works depicting other wars—including Stephen Crane's *The Red Badge of Courage,* Erich Maris Remarque's *All Quiet on the Western Front,* and Dalton Trumbo's *Johnny Got His Gun*—in exemplifying the soul-searing and life-draining nature of war. As Springsteen's soldier cowers in his bunker, his "finger on the trigger," not knowing whom he should trust, even his closest comrades and friends appear in his eyes as potential terrorists and enemies. Even when he looks into the eyes of his friend, Bobbie, he sees "just devils and dust." A deep dread pervades everything; the air seems filled with the fear of death.

But Springsteen's compassion here for the soldier under fire makes this song so much more than a partisan antiwar screed. Springsteen does not make the mistake here that so many made during Vietnam of confusing opposition to the war with contempt for those who were called upon to fight it. We empathize with the isolation and loneliness of those sent thousands of miles away from their homes and loved ones to implement a particular government policy. Without necessarily passing judgment on that policy, we long for the day when the soldier and his friends will no longer be "a long, long way from home," and when their fear will be banished and their devils exorcised.

It won't be an easy journey. "Devils & Dust" is palpable with the fear that comes from severing our connections to those things—those people, those ideals, those touchstones and verities—that give our lives their meaning and purpose. "I got God on my side," the soldier sings (knowing full well that those on the other side of the trenches are saying pretty much the same thing). "Got God on my side," Springsteen read as he analyzed the lyrics of "Devils and Dust" for the VH1 series *Storytellers*. Then he mused, "Who does not?"[9]

But God doesn't seem actually present to this young soldier out there in the desert. He seems all alone. "There is no greater evil than isolation," Springsteen said in an interview not long after *Devils & Dust* was released, echoing a point he had been making since (at least) *Nebraska*.[10]

The solider has a dream, a nightmare really. The dream conjures up visions of the valley of dry bones in the book of the prophet Ezekiel in the Hebrew Bible. But whereas in the biblical narrative God revives the bones of the dead and causes them to live again (Ezek. 37:5–6), in the soldier's dream in "Devils & Dust," the bones stay dead, and what rises from them is not new life but the stench of death. As Matthew Orel points out in his study "From Adam to Jesus: Springsteen's Use of Scripture," "Without God's intervention, bones do not come back to life, and people killed in battle stay dead. Biblical visions cannot tell the troops of today that God is, indeed, on their side."[11]

There will be no resurrection place down here in Springsteen's nightmare. There is no rising this time—not when "the things we do to survive kill the things we love," when the choices we make alienate us from the goodness that is within us and within creation. There is no rising when our actions cut us off from the "God-filled soul" with which, Springsteen asserts, we are born, but which we nurture, defend, and reclaim only with every life choice we make.

As the antidote to this all-pervasive fear and loathing, Springsteen posits not the certainty of ideology, or narrow patriotism, or even the call of a small and particular faith. It's not that faith—any faith—is wrong, but in times of deepest danger we need something more than religious creeds and partisan screeds. What then can banish the devils and dust, vanquish the specter of death that surrounds us, and restore our "God-filled souls"?

Only love can, Springsteen affirms. Only "the love that God wills." "So these three abide," Saint Paul wrote, "faith, hope, and love. And the greatest of these is love" (1 Cor. 13:13).

It is the love within us that moves us beyond hatred and fear and sets our hearts pumping again with the Spirit of God. Only when we approach life from the direction of love, and not from fear, do we reflect the divinity that is within our souls.

This is never an easy calling, and even the best of our human race answer it imperfectly. Most of us spend much of our time here lurching from mistake to mistake, occasionally saved by blessed moments of redemption, love, and grace. The great choice we face in life is whether to give in to the fear, or to seek to respond to life in a spirit of love; to live life in an attitude of hope, or to give in to the despair that we so often face.

A House on Higher Ground

Backstreets editor Christopher Phillips characterized the song "Devils & Dust" as "the album's overture,"[12] and it does set the stage for the characters we meet, the problems they face, and the choices they are called upon to make. "In every song on this record," Springsteen told the *New York Times,* "somebody's in some spiritual struggle between the worst of themselves and the best of themselves, and everybody comes out in a slightly different place. That thread runs through the record, and it's what gives the record its grounding in the spirit."[13]

Devils & Dust may be grounded in the spirit, as Springsteen says. But the men and women we meet there are hardly other-worldly. Rather, they are exceedingly down to earth, sometimes excessively, sometimes very crudely indeed. Their salvation, when it comes, arrives not through their escaping the world but through their living their lives fully and compassionately, here and now.

"I wanna build me a house, on higher ground," the singer in "Leah" exults. He wants to discover a world "where love's the only sound" and where the "shadow and doubt" of this mundane path we travel is no more. But he wants to do all this while still meeting his responsibilities and still feeling the physicality of life and love that the world offers. Moreover, he wants to do it side by side—or in the arms of—the one he loves, a woman named Leah. (Interestingly, Leah in the Bible is an outcast: the spurned wife of Jacob, who yearns for her more beautiful sister, Rachel. But in God's eyes, of course—as often, in Springsteen's—there are no outcasts. All men and women have their roles to play, both in the divine plan and in the great human epic.)

Leah's man does not hide from life: he lives it openly, with a hammer in one hand and a lantern in the other. He knows that he has the power to build or destroy—and both hammer and lantern can be used for either purpose, of course. The hammer can be a tool of destruction and violence, as well as construction and building. The lantern can be used to burn down, certainly, but it also can be used to enlighten and guide the way through darkness. The gifts we are given have no intrinsic value in and of themselves; it is our *choices* that render them either blessings or curses.

Deep living requires deep sharing: oftentimes, the deepest and most intimate sharing of body with body. "I'm gonna sleep tonight in Maria's bed," another character on *Devils & Dust* sings, invoking perhaps the greatest mother of all (Maria, Mary), but this time more as lover than as mother. The narrator of "Maria's Bed" has worked hard and his life isn't easy, but he's no complainer. He knows that hard work is the price he pays for survival. It's work he will do gladly if he knows that at the end of his labor he can "sleep tonight in Maria's bed."

There is no severe dichotomy here between the sacred and secular, no severe dualism between the pleasures of the flesh and the concerns of the soul. In such deep sharing between people obviously committed to one another there is a place both for body and for soul, both for sexuality and spirituality. The narrator yearns for Maria to hold tight his body—but only because she already embraces so lovingly his soul.

Maria bids him to join her in "the upper room": their lovers' chamber becomes a cenacle for a sweet feast of love. It is rather like an antechamber on the way toward heaven, a heaven they will find in each other's arms and bodies.

This man has learned that earthly riches are just so much "fools' gold" compared to the real riches that love brings. In the face of the faith he and Maria hold toward one another, all faiths learned secondhand seem leaden and earthbound. In the light of such deep reality, all other lights dim.

Not Even Close

Many were quick to ascribe the opening lyrics of "All the Way Home," with its reference to having failed "with the whole world lookin' on," to Springsteen's experience with the Kerry campaign. Such an interpretation overlooks the fact that this particular song was written in 1991.[14] In that earlier context, the song reflects more on the failure of Springsteen's first marriage than on his failure to help elect John Kerry to the presidency.[15] But, as always, Springsteen's cachet as a fellow failed mortal does help the words of the imperfect protagonist in "All the Way Home" to ring with a certain amount of authenticity.

This man is imperfect and knows it. He's not terribly happy about it. He certainly doesn't glory in his failures. But he accepts them as part of the price we all must pay for being alive in this world. He hasn't fully let go of his past failures: they linger, he says, like the "shadows and vapor" of a love that's gone (or, in a beautifully vivid image, they linger "like the shadow of that ring" the woman he's now courting *once* wore: she has obviously failed at marriage, as well).

They have both reached the point where they can either continue trudging sadly through life, or she can accept his offer and they can dance together for the rest of the night. They have to choose whether they will see their mutual imperfections as interpersonal Berlin Walls that separate and alienate them from each other, or whether they will see these failings as bridges between their beings, as common ground that they can use as a base for sharing their stories with one another, and learning from one another, and comforting one another.

But they have to act before it's too late. The bartender reminds them that it's "last call." For all of us, our own personal end times draw steadily a little closer with each passing hour. "Oh God, to have reached the point of death only to find that you have never lived at all," exclaimed Henry David Thoreau. "Without God, we cannot, but without us, God will not," Augustine once wrote, and without our commitment to act (whatever the risks of failure), there is no hope for us. Unless we dare to commit, and stick around for the long haul—and dare to take one another "all the way home"—our emotional lives will founder and sink.

This is what happens to the main character in "Reno," one of Bruce Springsteen's most controversial (and certainly most explicit) songs. "Reno" tells the story of a man's visit to a prostitute in no-sex-acts-barred detail (indeed, the "adult imagery" in the song made *Devils & Dust* the only Springsteen album ever to earn a parental advisory label). In "Reno" we learn that there is no such thing as grace on demand—that real grace comes not through casual relations and using others, but through the demands (and sometimes the limitations and sacrifice) of real lifelong commitment to one another. "Casual sex is a kind of closing the book of you," Springsteen told John Pareles from the *New York Times.* "Sex with somebody you love is opening the book of you, which is always a risky and frightening read."[16]

The prostitute and her john in "Reno" start off all right. She removes her nylons, and he holds them close to his face—an action that immediately sparks a remembrance of the lover he has lost. Grace arrives, but for the barest moment, before the woman has (in the most controversial line in the song) submitted her explicitly detailed list of fees. Whatever magic or excitement there might have been has been bludgeoned in the coarsest manner possible. However gentle and sensitive the prostitute's ministrations to her client now might be, he knows that this will be, at best, a business transaction.

The man's mind starts to drift, and he seeks emotional refuge in his memories of that genuine love he once had. Soon, he is back south of the border, by the side of the river in the Valle de des Rios—the Valley of Two Rivers—where the river of his life did indeed join and flow as one, for a time, with that of another human soul. He thinks of the sunlight in the beloved's hair, the blessed smell of fruit trees, the cool, refreshing water, the smile of his lover, which seemed to make everything right. It "was all I'd ever need," he thinks, yet it was "never really quite enough," and so their bond didn't survive.

The words of the prostitute call him back again to the "real" world. She pronounces him ready for action, completes the process of readying herself, then mounts him like a corpse. We are spared a description of their copulation but can imagine that it is mechanistic, efficient, and very quick.

When it's done, she pours her client a whisky and toasts him with the words "Here's to the best you ever had." But then, in the conclusion of the song, the man makes the obvious observation that it "wasn't the best" of anything in his life; it wasn't "even close." The real "best" for any of us is never gained on the cheap. It is, rather, that which costs us the most—in time, labor, and love. But it is also that which opens us to the true miracles of grace that abound when one soul commits itself to another. The real tragedy—for the main character in "Reno" and for so many of us— is that very often we only speak of these blessings in the past tense and are able to behold them only through the lens of memory.

Pockets Full of Dust

There are no guarantees of success in this life. Things can turn out badly for those who attempt to make a new start for themselves. But better it is, Springsteen thinks, to fail in the attempt to transcend the prisonlike surroundings in which we find ourselves than never to try at all. We have no guarantee of success. But if we do not try to move beyond the constraints of an oppressive life, then we do guarantee that sooner or later we will be numbered among its victims.

The surroundings faced by Rainey Williams, the chief character in "Black Cowboys," are bleak enough certainly, not to mention dangerous. A bright and precocious child, Rainey lives in the rundown Mott Haven neighborhood of the South Bronx.[17] Rainey comes home from school every day past the makeshift shrines of the children and youths who have been killed on the streets, whose "death and blood consecrated these places," Springsteen writes.

At home there is a protective, loving mother waiting for him, a mother whose worst fear is that Rainey will join the ranks of these child martyrs. She admonishes him to stay inside after school every day. She has fashioned him a protective cocoon, with television Westerns, and books about the black cowboys of the Old West, and plenty of maternal warmth and pride and joy. What Rainey lacks in stimuli from the outside world, he receives from her; in the midst of this decrepit exterior landscape (again likened by Springsteen to the valley of dry bones from Ezekiel), he has fashioned a vibrant interior one.

But in the heat of summer and the rains of fall, everything changes. Rainey loses his exclusive claim on his mother's attention and affection when she takes up with a successful neighborhood pimp, who moves in with Lynette and Rainey. He hides his money under the kitchen sink; Lynette gets hooked on drugs and spends more and more time asleep in bed. When Rainey lays his head on his mother's chest at night, it is as though he hears the specter of their past relationship in her heartbeat. That special relationship has now died, Rainey knows; he understands that the time has come for him to let go of childish things (including his mother's hand) and set out on his own adult journey.

He takes a wad of hundred dollar bills from the boyfriend's stash under the sink, kisses his sleeping mother farewell, and buys a ticket for a train headed west. Society may not honor his dreams, but Rainey will do all he can to make them real. As the train makes its way through Pennsylvania, Ohio, Indiana, then finally toward Oklahoma, Rainey is retracing that journey of those black cowboys of so long ago. Those brave men may be largely forgotten now, but their lives have enough energy in them to kindle new dreams, like the one that lives on in Rainey Williams.

There is no guarantee he will meet with worldly success. There is every assurance that his life will not be an easy one. He faces awesome obstacles, both of class and of race. The choices he will face will be stark; his only options will be surviving or not surviving. But for now, as this modern cowboy makes his way west, there is only the open road of possibility before him.

In another song, "Matamoros Banks," the possibility of a fortuitous ending has already vanished as the song begins. The narrator is already dead—drowned in the Rio Grande while trying to make his way into the United States from Mexico. His body now floats on the surface of the water, after having been submerged for two days. It is a grisly spectacle, and Springsteen pulls no punches in his descriptions of turtles eating away at the skin around the narrator's eyes, which now stare blankly toward the heavens.

But in spite of its starkness and tragedy, there is a tone of hope in "Matamoros Banks." The narrator has failed in his attempt to reach a new life across the border, yet there seems something nonetheless heroic in his attempt.

His physical life has ended, and even his body has largely been stripped away: "every trace" of who he once was physically now "is gone." But there is here no tone of regret or recrimination. Rather, it is a song of thanksgiving this man sings: not for the transient treasures of life, of which he had few, but for the abiding love of the one he hopes to reunite with again. The memory of the woman this man loves never leaves him; it is there every step of the way, as he trudges across the desert toward the border, as he sits alone in the wilderness at night, as he dives into the river to escape capture, as his soul ascends to meet the universe.

Springsteen has explicitly stated that he wrote "Matamoros Banks" as a sequel to "Across the Border" from *The Ghost of Tom Joad*.[18] But whereas that earlier song presented an ethereal vision of new life that could readily be interpreted as metaphorical,

"Matamoros Banks" presents an unambiguously physical picture of the challenges and risks such immigrants face in their journeys. For so many people the world over—including the hundreds who die every year on the Mexico-U.S. border—the great barrier to be faced, day in and day out, is not one of psychological well-being, or spiritual deepening, but one of sheer physical survival. In the severity of "Matamoros Banks," Springsteen attempts to capture some of the brutality of life lived on this sharpest and most unforgiving of edges.

Indeed, for the narrator of this song, "the things of the earth" have already made "their claim." He has paid a very high price and, no doubt given the rampant injustice of this world, an unfair price. Now he awaits "the things of heaven" to calculate their cost, and here he hopes, in the eternal reckoning of all things, that he will be vindicated and saved at last—if not on the physical banks of the Rio Grande, then across that great final river which all must cross and upon whose farther bank all who love will become one.

Mother, Behold Your Son

Perhaps the predominant theme of *Devils & Dust*—one that concerns fully five of the album's twelve songs—is the relationship of parents and their children, more explicitly (in four of the songs at least) the relationship of mothers and sons.

Springsteen's earlier work, of course, contained numerous references to troubled relationships between fathers and sons, reflecting no doubt his turbulent relationship with his own father. But as Springsteen has grown older and has moved beyond some of his earlier angst (and as he has fathered three children of his own), he seems willing to present a more balanced perspective on the parent-child bond and even to portray some of the positive gifts our parents provide us—such as love, nurture, and protection. Especially critical for Springsteen is the bond children develop with their mothers. Springsteen has called mothers "the soul protectors" of their children.[19] But when that bond between them is severed, the results can be calamitous.

In "Silver Palomino," a young boy whose mother has died has a vision of a stunning white horse running through the hills his mother loved so much. Everything about those hills is now a memory for the boy, a steady recounting of all the places and things so immutably identified with his mother. Likewise, the spectral horse captures so much of the boy's mother's essence as well: the horse's moon-reflected coat of "frosted diamonds" captures his mother's beauty; her unchainable power reminds him of his mother's strength. The scent of the winter that must come releases within the boy's memory the precious scent of his mother's skin, to which he was pressed and held close many times, no doubt.

But then, he also remembers that summer when all was dry, and the grazing lands withered, and his mother's hand slipped from his own. And then, she was gone. And he knew that now there was a brand new journey into unknown hills for him to make—alone. He must continue this journey accompanied only by the dream of a beautiful white horse and the memories of a beautiful woman who will never be vanquished and never be forgotten.

In "Jesus Was an Only Son," Springsteen explores perhaps the most famous mother-son relationship of all, finally taking us to Calvary itself. By far the most explicitly religious of all Springsteen's songs, "Jesus Was an Only Son" is a reverent, almost hymnlike ode to Jesus of Nazareth and his mother, Mary. Its lyrics and music could almost come right out of a mainline Christian hymnbook.

The bond between the two is deep, and their destinies are linked. We see Mary walking beside her son as he moves toward the cross, but then we flashback to Jesus as a child sitting at his mother's feet, learning the lessons of their Jewish faith. Theirs is a seamless mother-child bond, and they complement each other perfectly and fully. Mary has nurtured Jesus, instructed him, and sent him forth into the world. Now through his ministry and his death, he will show all people the pathway to God.

At Gethsemane, with his own death beckoning, Jesus experiences his humanity intensely. He understands fully all the gifts of worldly existence that will now be barred from him. He knows the choice he is making and why he is making it. "That's what makes

our choices have meaning—the things that we sacrifice," Springsteen said as he introduced this song in St. Paul in May 2005.[20]

"If God can become human," Thomas Aquinas wrote, "then that
teaches us that the things of this earth can become reflections of
the holy." Within this life, we, like the human Jesus, face all of
those losses that can "never be replaced" and those destinations we
will never reach. But through the divine light glowing in his face
and in his heart, our way to God is illuminated at last and that wide
chasm between God and humankind is finally bridged.

In an earlier verse of the song, a mother comforts her child as
she bids him to sleep. By the end of "Jesus Was an Only Son," the
son is comforting his mother as he dries her tears and reminds her
that, whatever the vexations of the world, as long as God reigns all
will be well.

Remember, Jesus tells his mother, "the soul of the universe"—his
Father in heaven—"willed a world and it appeared." It is as though
Jesus is proclaiming, "This is my Father's world," in spite of all the
pain and loss we experience here. In spite of all the evil things people do to the earth and to one another, "God reigns; let the earth be
glad!" Be glad, as the old hymn says, hold tight to hope, and know
that beating at the very soul of the universe is a divine will that offers
to all of us gifts of grace and mercy too numerous to tell.

The Ties That Bind—or Don't

Of course, not all mother-son relationships meet the heights of that
exemplified by Jesus and Mary. Such may be the ideal of the Christian tradition, but it represents a mark from which many fall far
short. In "The Hitter," a man's relationship with his mother has
broken down completely, to the extent that she won't even let him
into her house. He is forced to confess the sins of his life through
his mother's screen door, as desperately he implores her to "just
open the door" and let him come in and lie down. He senses, perhaps, that if he can't find at least minimal relief in the abode of his
own mother, he must be truly doomed. If his mother won't provide
him with sanctuary, then who on earth will?

He's a latecomer in seeking maternal approbation, however. He was largely abandoned as a child—put on a riverboat to escape the police and told to fend for himself. He took up a trade that came easy to him: if he was going to get in fights anyway, he figured he might as well get paid for it, so he became a boxer. He was a success—a champion—for a time. He became known as a vicious hitter who would show no mercy, who would pummel his opponents to the brink of death.

But if, as Jesus said in the Beatitudes, it is the merciful who will obtain mercy, then it stands to reason that those who show no mercy to others aren't going to find clemency when they need it either. "The Hitter" has chosen a life where all those who cross his path are, ipso facto, his sworn enemies. "The hand of the dyer is stained by the dye which it works," the Buddha is said to have pronounced, in introducing the fifth step along the Noble Eightfold Path to enlightenment—that of "right livelihood." There are certain occupations that are simply incompatible with spiritual advancement, the Buddha believed. We can never hope to find spiritual fulfillment if we spend all of our waking hours engaged in professions that harm others and kill the spirit. The Buddha named professions such as slave trader, poison dealer, and caravan trader. No doubt, boxer could be on that list, as well.

With his career now over, the one who would not show mercy knows nothing but the endless cycle of violence and despair. Jesus warned that those who live by the sword would perish by the sword. Perhaps some people, like this boxer, are doomed as soon as they take up the sword in the first place.

For others, the blessed moment of *metanoia*—change of heart—finally arrives. Sometimes, as the song title indicates, that change is a "Long Time Comin.'"

In "Long Time Comin,'" Springsteen ponders the demands of family—and of fatherhood in particular. The main character in the song thinks back upon his own absent father. His father was "just a stranger," he says; he was "somebody I'd see around"—words applicable to a father who was physically absent, of course, but also to one who was emotionally absent in spite of his physical presence. The singer realizes how much that absence has wounded him and how it has created a certain emptiness in his soul that he has carried around since.

He vows that he will not inflict this wound on his own children. Life is hard enough if we have to answer for our own mistakes, without having to carry around the sins visited upon us by earlier generations. As he feels the little child below him tugging on his shirt, he senses the ties that bind him to those he has sired. In a flash, he realizes what a precious burden this is. He vows to honor the trust life has pushed on him: finally—right now—at this critical point in the life he leads, he pledges to "bury [his] old soul and dance on its grave."

That night, the man lies awake beneath open skies and the humbling glories of the Cassiopeia and Orion constellations. As his family sleeps undisturbed with him in the open air, he reaches across and feels the new life stirring in his wife's belly. He knows that the future holds hope. But he knows, too, that a good part of that future, for these little ones at least, depends on him. "I ain't gonna fuck it up this time," he vows to the silent cosmos; it is a prayer for strength from a decent man's heart, now carved on his own conscience and duly registered in heaven.

We make mistakes in life, more than we care to number sometimes. But faith tells us that we can know times of grace and redemption as well. Often those times take forever to arrive, and our journeys toward wholeness may be long ones, and the landmarks of our souls not always pleasant to contemplate. But as Saint Augustine once advised, each of us must pray like everything depends on God, and work like everything depends on us. Our lives are not bound interminably to failure and despair. Sometimes grace may seem a long time in coming, and we'll all receive our share of knocks and bruises before that moment of redemption finally gets here. But the fact that grace arrives at all is, truly, amazing—and the choicest of all blessings for which we can ever hope.

Chapter Twelve

Coming Home Again
Magic

*I*n 1941, publisher Henry Luce posted an editorial in *Life* magazine, his leading publication. It called for the establishment of "the
first great American Century." It was time, Luce said, for the United
States to move beyond the isolationist legacy that had dogged it
since the end of the First World War. America's calling now lay,
Luce declared, in establishing itself as the world's preeminent
power, a shining beacon of hope, freedom, and opportunity.

Standing now a little more than a half century from Luce's stirring pronouncement, the remnant of such a heroic banner seems to
lie in tatters. Where once our leaders could plausibly speak of it
being "morning in America," now to many—including Bruce
Springsteen—all seems dark and drear. It seems as though night
and fog have descended on this "last lone American night."

Groping our way through that darkness—while at the same time
pondering what might have been and what might come next in our
collective story—is the overriding theme of *Magic*, a full-throttle
rocker Springsteen recorded with the entire E Street Band at
Southern Tracks in Atlanta during the spring of 2007. Brendan
O'Brien once again served as producer, and the album was
released in the United States in late September.

Magic's recurrent image is *finding our way back home*—as individuals and (especially, perhaps) as a nation. If *The Rising* was
Springsteen's response to the terror and tragedy of September 11,
then *Magic* contains his ruminations on the years that have come

since. It is certainly an understatement to say that he doesn't like what he sees.

Is Anybody Alive Out There?

In "Radio Nowhere," the first song on the album, Springsteen bemoans the kind of mass culture and mass thought against which George Orwell fulminated in his 1946 essay "Politics and the English Language." "If thought corrupts language, then language can also corrupt thought," Orwell wrote, and as it is for language, so too is it for other aspects of our culture.[1] Mass culture can have an anesthetizing effect on the mind of a civilization.

Mass commercial culture—free of spontaneity and real diversity and its own "rhythm"—is, for Springsteen, both the cause and the symbol of our present malaise. He's trying to find his way home, he sings in the very first line of the album. He spins the radio dial to find that song to guide him home, but all he hears is "a drone" that bounces off a satellite, as though filling the very air; it is as though the atmosphere itself has become militarized. Even the sacred strains of rock and roll now answer the call of some central authority, rather than the spontaneous calling of its own rhythm.

"Is there anybody alive out there?" Springsteen asks over and over, desperately, as he sings into the void and darkness. Has anyone been left alive? Or have we all become deadened spirits, nothing but lost numbers in a file?

He continues to make his way through the darkness, seeking for lost soul mates, wanting more than anything to hear again the rhythm of life. He yearns for the diversity and abundance that makes life worth living: he wants to hear the clash of guitars, the beat of drums, the blessed cacophony of countless voices "speaking in tongues."

As always (or at least almost always) in Springsteen, despair doesn't get the last word. Even here his vision abides, and his search continues. Even as he gropes about in the darkness of nighttime in America, Springsteen says he's looking for a "mystery train"—an allusion both to Elvis Presley's "train I ride, sixteen coaches long," promising personal contentment and romantic love, and to that blessed train of unity and transformation which leads us to that land of hope and dreams of which Springsteen has sung often in recent years.

As do many Americans, Springsteen believes that our train has fallen off its track. The cause of our great national derailment has been the war in Iraq and the culture of manipulation and deceit that has spawned it. Getting that train heading toward home again is the concern of the rest of the songs on *Magic*.

Somebody Made a Bet, Somebody Paid

The war is never far away in any of the songs on *Magic*, either as background and context, or often more explicitly, as part of the album's narrative chord.

"Who'll be the last to die for a mistake?" Springsteen asks in one song, directly echoing the words of John Kerry, as a Vietnam veteran testifying before Congress in 1971. "We are asking Americans to think about that because how do you ask a man to be the last man to die in Vietnam?" Kerry asked at the time. "How do you ask a man to be the last man to die for a mistake?"[2]

To Springsteen, the truth about both Vietnam and Iraq are obvious, as are the deadly consequences of such grievous errors in judgment and policy. The blood of the innocent will again be spilled; grief will again cover the land. "Last to Die" is an angry song, full of references to wise men really being fools, and cities in flames, and tyrants and kings being strung up at the city gates. Springsteen (like so many of us) looks out at this ill-conceived, absurd war, and asks (as Pete Seeger did years before) "When will we ever learn? When will we ever learn?"

But Springsteen's work rises above the level of mere polemic through his ability to amplify his opposition to the war in Iraq by presenting in moving human detail the real tragedy the war has wrought.

In "Gypsy Biker," he tells of one soldier's homecoming—in a casket. Again, the initial tone of the song is angry: the war has enriched various speculators and profiteers, and no one will speak the awful truth of a war fought for oil and of those who make lots of money through the deaths of their fellow countrymen. But the anger gives way to resignation, emotional numbness, and the self-destruction of despair.

But even if the world doesn't seem to care about the demise of this "Gypsy Biker," his family and friends do. They take the dead soldier's cherished motorcycle out of the garage and polish off the chrome. They then drive it to the outskirts of town, into the foothills, and in a grand gesture like at a Viking's funeral, they set it afire in a blazing testament to the one they've lost, a mighty conflagration of anger and of love.

But when the winds die down, and the fire merely smolders, and the world lurches on, then all that will remain is the void—the empty space where this lost soldier once stood. In the emptiness, those left behind will continue to founder, locked in self-destruction, especially that of drugs and alcohol. The casualties of war are not merely those killed on the battlefield.

Nor are the only casualties on the battlefield those who are killed. In "Devil's Arcade" Springsteen sings of another soldier come home—this one not in a casket but on a stretcher. In addition to the almost four thousand American troops killed in Iraq as of this writing, there have been an estimated thirty thousand other casualties—some of whom have been maimed, physically and emotionally, for life.[3] This has been one of the great "unspoken" tragedies of this terrible war. "Devil's Arcade" is Springsteen's attempt to give voice to these victims.

Perhaps the soldier here is the same frightened young man from "Devils & Dust." Now back home, he dreams about earlier, happier days of romance and camaraderie. Those are all gone now—shattered by his being called upon to pay the price of someone else's "bet"—someone else's misguided and arrogant policy. The war came, and with it the great tragic transformation of this solder's life and thousands of others.

Now there is no more lovemaking, no more "evenings of perfume and gin," no more campside poker games, no more heroism.

There is just the blue-walled hospital ward, swirling around him like an unnamed sea, where this young, maimed warrior now lies adrift with the other victims of Iraq's "devil's arcade."

But even here in such a sad place, there is hope; there is the glimmer of "something like faith." His beloved whispers to the soldier that she's there with him, and she dares him to dream about tomorrow. She dares him to recall that normal life they once lived: their quiet house, the smell of breakfast cooking in the kitchen, the glorious moment of feeling alive, with the new morning's sun warming his cheek. She dares him to hope for something like resurrection, for a new rising. She dares him to ride each moment—each heartbeat—toward a future that still waits, in spite of everything, a future where love's rhythm can vanquish at last the bitterness and fear of the devil's arcade.

We'll Be Comin' Down

There is a plaintive quality to some of the songs on *Magic*, as though Springsteen seems to be asking, "How did we as a nation fall so far, so fast?" He believes that there is plenty of blame to go around, and he hurls the choicest bits of it at those currently in power. "You can't kill your way to security, and you can't lead through scaring people," he told Joe Levy from *Rolling Stone*. "Maybe you can get people to vote for you sometimes, but it's not a tactic that's going to provide the kind of moral authority and leadership that it's going to take to communicate in the world. It's the coward's way out." [4]

But in a democracy none of us are blameless. "Your own worst enemy has come to town," Springsteen sings in another song, and as the character in the *Pogo* comic strip proclaimed while looking out at the garbage dump of a world before him, "We have met the enemy, and he is us."

A society truly at ease with itself—that knows what it is and that has a shining image of its liberty and its responsibilities deeply imprinted in its being—isn't afraid to face challenges, criticisms, and even fundamental reformation. It makes change its friend, not its enemy. It doesn't have to remove all of its mirrors so that it doesn't have to see itself accurately (as the rest of the world sees it).

But a society that ignores the dark side of its history and refuses to know itself is constantly under siege, more from within perhaps than without. The high-sounding ideals it articulates are just words. Its flag is debased; it has become just a piece of cloth, mere detritus carried away by the wind.

Similarly, in "Livin' in the Future" there seems to be nothing overhead but the blue, cloudless skies of denial. Things are falling apart and ill winds are blowing, but the singer doesn't want to hear about it. He just wants to go on, acting as though all is fine. In spite of a whole catalogue of problems and catastrophes, he tells his mate not to worry and not to fret, because "we're livin' in the future, and none of this has happened yet."

But the illusion of a future based upon falsehood is nevertheless a lie. As much as the singer might want to kid himself into oblivion with the concluding "na na na's," sooner or later the center will not hold any longer and there will be a reckoning.

As often in Springsteen's work, you can listen to a song like "Livin' in the Future" either in a personal or political key: either as a warning to an arrogant individual to change his or her ways, or as a judgmental prophecy hurled at a nation mired in vainglory. One interpretation does not preclude the other. But throughout *Magic,* Springsteen manages to include a phrase here, an allusion there, to nudge us into understanding that there is something more than purely personal trials and tribulations under consideration here.

In "Livin' in the Future" there are Bush-era references to grey skies on Election Day, strutting cowboys, and authoritarian jackboots. Likewise, in another song, when Springsteen sings, "You'll be coming down now, baby," he could, of course, simply be issuing a warning from one who knows that material possessions and worldly success do not bring happiness. Or, as is more likely in the context of this particular album, he might also be chronicling the inevitable fall of a society rich in things but poor in soul.

This Is What Will Be

The album's title track is yet another frightening exploration of these Orwellian times in which we live. "The song 'Magic,'" Springsteen told *Rolling Stone,* is about "living in a time when anything that is true can be made to seem like a lie, and anything that is a lie can be made to seem true." He then quoted the words of one of President Bush's advisors to a reporter from the *New York Times:* "We make our own reality," this advisor said openly. "You guys report it. [But] we make it."[5]

"Trust none of what you hear," "Magic" reminds us, "and less of what you'll see." Then, hauntingly, it proclaims, "This is what will be."

Sounding like a carnival huckster (or an American politician) Springsteen introduces us to a whole bag of manipulative tricks. There are hidden coins, and cards up his sleeve, and of course, the ever popular rabbit pulled out of a hat.

But then, things turn more sinister, and the fake magician is soon singing of slipping the shackles on his wrist ("probably the most potent global symbol of today's USA," one writer has said),[6] and escaping a chained box in the river like Houdini. Then he turns his "magic" against his listeners and cheerily asks for a volunteer to saw in half with his "shiny saw blade." When this is finally done, the magician's work will be completed and our very freedom will be gone. And the strange fruit of this dark magic will be that awful future spawned by the passionate intensity of the worst of human nature and the low ebb of our own history.

The Vision Abides

Only a nation that has ideals can lament falling from them. Shortly after the release of *Magic,* Springsteen told CBS's *60 Minutes* that his purpose was to "chart the distance between American ideals and American reality." [7] In the frankly romantic, lushly nostalgic "Girls in Their Summer Clothes," Springsteen reintroduces us to ourselves as a country. With music that could have been written and played by the Beach Boys, he portrays an idyllic summer, a moment when everything seems right.

Lovers holding hands promenade beneath the streetlights along a boulevard aptly named Blessing Avenue. The little rituals of domestic contentment proceed unmolested. There is no darkness on the edge of town here, but rather the shining, friendly lights at Frankie's Diner. Coffee cups get endlessly refilled, and abundance and prosperity are everywhere. There's an air of hope and optimism, a "can do" attitude of a people who know who they are.

But no dreams last forever, much less dreams as idealized and romantic as these. "The girls in their summer clothes" may be beautiful, but they are also the ones who pass the singer by. He sings of a love affair that has ended; a harsher reality has started to intrude into this "perfect" tableaux. Maybe this next girl will be the one, the singer hopes. As long as he still has his feet, he can join in the dance; perhaps it is a "fool's dance." But can we do anything but join in the life-giving whirl of it all?

Simply daydreaming of what has been gets us nowhere. Simply hoping for what we want won't make it happen. Simply wishing for a good outcome does not turn our hopes into reality. Another song, "I'll Work for Your Love," reminds us that real life—real love—means real work.

Bruce Springsteen is a man of deep faith whose spiritual and religious values seldom lie far beneath the surface of his work. But his is a markedly nontraditional, deeply embodied, fully incarnated faith. Springsteen would agree with the biblical declaration that "by their fruits you shall know them" (Matt. 7:16). He would probably also agree that if our professions of faith are to have real worth, there needs to be no small measure of heart and hand—and real effort—behind them.

In "I'll Work for Your Love," Springsteen presents a veritable smorgasbord of religious symbols: stations of the cross, crowns of thorns, books of Revelation, rosary beads, temples of bones, pieces of the cross, the garden of Eden, even "seven drops of blood" (an apparent reference to Lev. 16:19).[8] But these trappings of religion rise and fall—are redeemed or discarded—only insofar as the real man and real woman in this song choose to act upon them and make them real. Any *outer* ritual (a remnant of faith, a profession of love) must be matched by an *inner* reference point in order to ring true.

There is never a free lunch in Springsteen's songs. Perhaps, in his worldview, there is no such thing as a free gift of grace, either. Others may want something for nothing, the man sings to his Theresa, but "I'll work for your love," he tells her. I'll do what I need to do to make our faith in our life together—our hope for the future, our love for one another—become a living presence in this all too real world.

This Is Our Hometown

Getting back to where we need to be will not be easy. "It's gonna be a long walk home," one of the album's final songs predicts. "Long Walk Home" begins with the narrator standing on a doorstep, trying to understand why things have gone wrong. Given Springsteen's deep concern for the direction in which American life and politics seen headed, it is not illogical to picture him here at the base of the Statue of Liberty—at our great national doorstep—trying to begin again the journey toward America as it should be. Things look bleak, but the world goes on: in the refulgence of summer, as Emerson said, it is still a luxury to draw the breath of life. The stars above still cast their benediction over all. In the distance, the singer's hometown beckons—with its memories and maybe even with its hopes.

As the singer tours his hometown again, much has been taken: the veterans' hall stands deserted, and no shining light of friendship glows from the diner in this town (in stark contrast to the one in "Girls in Their Summer Clothes"). Even here, in his hometown, no one knows this man anymore, and he recognizes no one. He seems surrounded by "rank strangers" now. The sign on the diner—"Gone"—could also apply to the lifeblood of this place.

But even if this is the way things are, it need not be the way things have to be. "This is what will be," Springsteen sang on "Magic" as he presented his frightening vision of the world that is to come. But remember Scrooge in Dickens's *Christmas Carol,* as the Ghost of Christmas Future (the most frightening ghost of all) finally finishes with him: "Assure me," Scrooge implores the spirit, "that I yet may change these shadows you have shown me, by an altered life?"

"Long Walk Home" gives us hope that we may wipe away the writing on the stone and redeem our national honor and purpose. We can, through our own honest efforts, recreate that place where the light still shines and neighbors and friends abide and help each other. We can discern for ourselves, and for our country, our "reason to begin again."

When the singer's father expresses to his son his pride in being born in such a "beautiful" place, he's not talking about either scenic wonders or quaint picturesqueness. He's not speaking about any well-manicured gated communities or prosperous, isolated, high-achiever ghettos. He's speaking about common, everyday places like Freehold (where Springsteen actually was born), or like Cleveland, or like Flint, Michigan, or Youngstown, Pennsylvania, or like the Ninth Ward of New Orleans. He's speaking about any of the thousands upon thousands of cities and towns and boroughs and villages, large and small, all across this country that common, everyday Americans call home.

These are the places that won't let us go and that remind us what it means to be Americans. It means standing up for freedom, and taking care of one another, and making sure that everyone has a fair shake and an equal chance. It means making sure that people play by the rules, tell the truth, pay a fair day's wage for a fair day's work, and do their best, and never give up. It's about knowing our history well, admitting when we've been wrong, and attempting to make up for it. It's about casting the circle of love and freedom as wide as possible, and finding a place for everyone at the table. And it's about knowing—really knowing—that it's never too late to begin again. It's never too late to make that great turn and come back home.

Being an American means knowing that certain values *are* "set in stone." If we turn our backs on them, we tear away a huge part of our national soul. With Langston Hughes, Bruce Springsteen is asking us to "Let America be America again." He's imploring us to uncover our lights and let them shine—to become beacons of hope and courage to one another along the way of our long journey back toward the homeland of our hearts.

Conclusion

Bruce's Ten ~~Commandments~~ *Suggestions*
for Spiritual Living ^

*T*here is no ultimate authority for interpreting the "real" meaning of any of Springsteen's lyrics. Even Springsteen himself is often refreshingly vague when it comes to explaining precisely what some of his songs mean. Much of the power of Springsteen's work—like any decent art—emerges only from the resonance it creates in the soul of the observer. The angle from which we look at something changes it completely. Whether or not Springsteen's words reverberate with some particular meaning for us depends to a great degree on what we bring to our conversation with them: how they reflect (or don't) our experience, outlook, and aspiration. If there is a "religion" of Springsteen, then it is certainly one that places great importance on individual freedom of belief.

Likewise, saying (as this book does) that there is a "gospel" according to Bruce Springsteen—some good news that this world of ours fails to hear (and heed) at its peril—is not the same as saying that Springsteen presents, in his writings, any sort of systematic (or even especially consistent) theology. He does not present a systematic theology (as the singer in "Reno" might add, "not even close"). In his deeply perceptive essay "The Catholic Imagination of Bruce Springsteen," Father Andrew Greeley marvels at how "naturally" and "unself-consciously" Springsteen invokes concepts such as prayer, heaven, and God.[1] But in many of Springsteen's songs, of course, matters like prayer seem the farthest thing from people's minds; the locus of the action is just this dust beneath our feet, and God is nowhere to be found (or heard from) and is either "drifting in heaven" or has been thrust aside in favor of more earthly concerns.

There is within the Springsteen canon neither the consistency of doctrine for which a staunch creedalist might hope, nor sufficient hermeneutical density to please a professor of theology. Nonetheless, Springsteen's assembled works do present "good tidings" to those who hear them. As we listen to Springsteen, certain themes of hope, joy, and challenge emerge clearly:

1. The world has gone awry. "You and I know what this world can do," Bruce sings on "If I Shall Fall Behind." It's often not very pretty. The ceremonies of innocence are often drowned before the raging waters of life, and we have all, in a sense, been lost in the flood. The world according to Springsteen is often portrayed as a gritty, conflicted, oftentimes dark and sinister place. It differs for the particular characters involved in each song, of course, but the darkness is always there on the edge of things, or not very far beneath the surface.

2. There is a power within the souls of men and women to transcend the world, and to achieve real victories in spite of the world. When Springsteen sang Dylan's "Chimes of Freedom" in East Berlin in 1988, he sang of all the "countless confused, accused, misused, strung-out ones and worse." His own songs contain as vast an array of those whom life has broken. But for all of them, there are also those whom life has tried but who yet refuse to cower. For every homeless loser who has left his wife and kids high and dry back in Baltimore, there is that good man or good woman who works endlessly at a thankless job to meet his or her responsibilities. People have within them the power to choose to be true to themselves and what really matters.

3. The world is as it is. There is both great pain and great joy in life, Springsteen affirms. Once we have accepted that the pain is part of the deal, then we are free to experience genuine joy when it comes our way. "Life is difficult," wrote M. Scott Peck in the opening of his bestseller *The Road Less Traveled.* "Bad news is a fact of life," agrees no less an ebullient figure than the Dalai Lama. Don't look for all good news or all bad news in Springsteen's songs, because you're going to find both, in abundance.

4. *Life without connections is empty and dangerous.* What an amazing assortment of "whores and gamblers," not to mention "lost souls," populates the lines of Springsteen's songs. From the tough-talking thug in "Meeting Across the River" all the way to the lonely john in "Reno," Springsteen sings of a stark array of misfits, criminals, and losers. But there is always compassion in the portraits he presents, and we sense that the line between winners and losers is a narrow one, and that what differentiates the former from the latter are the connections they have with other people. Isolation kills, Springsteen declares; it kills the soul even more certainly than the body.

5. *Our stories symbolize something deeper.* The great lie of our contemporary, celebrity-crazed culture is that only the rich and famous have stories worth telling. We are led to believe that the life experience of the rest of us "regular" men and women isn't terribly significant, So, we deprecate our own experience; we dismiss it or ignore it altogether. We look elsewhere (to the tabloids, or television, or to outside "experts") to tell us what's really important. Springsteen's work stands as perhaps our culture's most forceful and persistent challenge to this great lie. (This is, perhaps, the reason for much of his enduring popularity.) There are almost no celebrities featured in Springsteen's songs (Jesus, Mary, maybe an occasional appearance by Elvis). His stories are *our* stories, and the wisdom (as well as the folly) they contain are ours too.

6. *Life is embodied.* There is in Springsteen no strict dichotomy between body and soul, no denigration of human sexuality, no minimizing the importance of physical intimacy in the development of a healthy, whole being. In Springsteen's songs, sex is often presented as an important manifestation of the deeper knowing of one person and another; it can be a living sacrament, a visible sign of the deeper union of two souls. On the other hand, an unjust relationship will manifest itself in a debased, exploitive, or lifeless sexuality. Sexuality is intrinsically neither good nor evil, Springsteen implies; here, as in all human ventures, only good soil will produce worthy fruit.

7. It's all about change. "Ooh . . . growin' up," Bruce sang way back on *Greetings from Asbury Park, N.J.* introducing us to but the first chapter of his own life's saga. Another reason for the durability of the hold he has on many of his fans is that his music has grown up with him. The Springsteen who sang on *Greetings* is physically, of course, the same person who sings on *Magic*. But far different are those albums' perspectives from one another (and both differ much from, say, *Tunnel of Love*). Springsteen's later works reverberate from a different time and place than his earlier efforts, but they in no way abandon or annul them. In being true to the place where he is *now*, at this time of his life (thereby encouraging all of us to do so as well), Springsteen honors his past, affirms it, and then moves beyond it. If we cling to the past, it withers and dies. If we let it go gracefully and move on to the next stage of our lives, the gifts of the past can continue to bless us.

8. There is no guarantee of success. Often the tender ones will be crushed, and evil will seem to have triumphed. Like the seeds sewn by the hardworking migrant workers in "This Hard Land," many of our well-meaning and even heartfelt efforts will not bear fruit.[2] They will seem to lie fallow on the ground, discarded along the wayside of life. There is often in life no easy treasure to be found, no pot of gold waiting for us just over the horizon. Whatever various New Age gurus might tell us, the universe is not just a catalogue from which we get to pick and choose all the things we want for ourselves. Sometimes life teaches us lessons about humility and silence and emptiness and pain and unanswered prayers. At those times, we know that our true treasure is the power of our own integrity, and our reward lies in keeping faith with those other decent, down-to-earth, hardworking people everywhere.

9. Hope is resilient. The Czech playwright and former president Vaclav Havel once said that hope is not the assurance that things will be easy or will work out well. Rather, he said, hope is the deep inner assurance (a "dimension of the human spirit," he calls it) that what we are doing makes sense and has purpose and that it is the right thing to do, whatever the immediate consequences. The men and women in Springsteen's songs may win or they may lose, but they seldom abandon all hope. Despair is seldom, if ever, given the final word. The hope these characters exhibit is not blind optimism, detached from the realities of life. They have seen and experienced too much to believe in any sort of pie-in-the-sky utopianism. True, deep hope is not some kind of childish fantasy we refuse to shake, whatever happens to us. Rather, real and durable hope is born from real life; it is born on the vortex between the world as it is and as it ought to be. Life is lived on the cusp between hope and history. It is hope that carries us human ones on the sacred vector toward life's divine possibilities.

10. There is always something more. Bruce Springsteen is widely credited as one of the outstanding storytellers of our time. Many of his songs are rich in tangible details of life here and now: the factory whistle blowing, the streets of the city on fire, the empty space beside us in the bed. But if Bruce is luminous in his work, shining a light of perception on the horizontal dimension of this earthly life, so he is also numinous, casting this life we lead in the brilliance of an almost mystic glow and shedding the radiance of discernment on that vertical beam which crashes through the linear plane of existence and points it toward that which is higher, deeper, somehow transcendent. "The invariable mark of wisdom," Ralph Waldo Emerson once said, "is to see the miraculous in the common."

As Springsteen's career has developed through the 1970s onward into the twenty-first century, he has emerged as many things to many people: respected musician, A-list celebrity, commercial juggernaut, progressive political spokesman, even (judging from his recent work with the Seeger Sessions Band) protector of the American musical heritage. But however varied Springsteen's endeavors have become, all have been empowered by a deep-seated sense of the profound worth and meaning inherent in this life we lead.

Springsteen himself has spoken of the "incredible internal landscape" that his Catholic faith bequeathed to him, and how parochial education awakened in him "a powerful world of potent imagery that became alive and vibrant and vital." This internal world was often frightening, he admitted, but it also "held out the promises of ecstasies and paradise."[3] Out of these fears—and out of these divine promises—the songs of a lifetime have ushered forth.

In his willingness to explore his own internal landscape, Bruce Springsteen leads all of us who hear him toward exploring our own. He reminds us that we are not alone, in the universe or upon this earth, and that we do not live for ourselves alone. Springsteen calls upon us to keep faith with the oppressed and marginalized wherever they may cross our paths. In so doing, we answer clearly the calling of prophetic men and women of all times who sought to live out their dreams of a reign of justice, peace, and love, on earth as in heaven.

The essence of Springsteen's good news is not just that there is a power which moves through human history transcending differences, liberating that which lies captive, and healing all wounds. His even better news is that this divine power lives and moves through indisputably common, fallible, imperfect people like us. Through the words and music of Bruce Springsteen may our ears be opened to the Spirit's song all about us, may our eyes be opened to the Spirit's gifts deep within us, and may our hands and hearts be opened to do the Spirit's work here in the midst of this confusing, conflicted, mysterious, amazing world.

Notes

Introduction: The Ministry of Rock and Roll

1. Renee Graham, "The Boss Rules (The Man, That Is)," *Boston Globe*, August 13, 2002, E1.

2. Joseph Campbell, *The Power of Myth* (New York: Doubleday, 1988), 5.

3. For the complete listing, see http://www.brucespringsteen.net/songs/index.html.

4. Bruce Springsteen, *Songs* (New York: Avon Books, 1998).

5. Fred Norris, "Bruce Springsteen Delivers on 'Promise,'" *VH1.com*, March 22, 1999, http://www.vh1.com/artists/news/512970/19990322/springsteen_bruce. jhtml.

Chapter 1: Welcome to the Fall

1. For a very thorough chronology of Springsteen's life through 2003, see June Skinner Sawyers, ed., *Racing in the Street: The Bruce Springsteen Reader* (New York: Penguin Books, 2004), xix–xxiv.

2. Daniel Wolff, *Fourth of July, Asbury Park: A History of the Promised Land* (New York: Bloomsbury, 2005), 171.

3. Springsteen, *Songs,* 6.

4. Bruce Springsteen, *VH1 Storytellers: Bruce Springsteen*, DVD (New York: Columbia Music Video, 2005).

5. See Caryn Rose, "Somerville Nights," *Backstreets*, Winter 2002/Spring 2003, 19.

6. Lester Bangs, review of *Greetings from Asbury Park, N.J., Rolling Stone*, July 5, 1973, http://www.rollingstone.com/reviews/album/107193/review/ 5943460/ greetingsfromasburyparknj.

7. Bruce Springsteen, "The Rolling Stone Interview: Bruce Springsteen," by Kurt Loder, *Rolling Stone*, December 6, 1984, reprinted in Editors of Rolling Stone, *Bruce Springsteen: The Rolling Stone Files* (New York: Hyperion, 1996), 153.

8. Wolff, *Fourth of July*, 171.

9. Rich Lynch, Laura Lynch, and Pat Cacioppo, "Bruce Springsteen Rehearsals: These Shows Are Paramount Performances," *Kweevak.com Music*

Magazine, April 28, 2005, http:// www.kweevak.com/rd_art_2005_04_28 _springsteen.php.

10. Dave Marsh, *Born to Run: The Bruce Springsteen Story,* vol. 1 (New York: Thunder's Mouth Press, 1996), 50.

11. Sean O'Casey, quoted in *Wisdom Quotes: Quotations to Inspire and Challenge,* http://www.wisdomquotes.com/002549.html.

12. Marsh, *Born to Run,* 53.

Chapter 2: Creating Community

1. Springsteen, *Songs,* 23.

2. For the shifting makeup of the E Street Band and the makeup of Springsteen's other groups, between 1965 and 2004, see Sawyers, *Racing in the Street,* xi–xii.

3. Springsteen, *Songs,* 25.

4. Ibid., 26.

5. A very thorough listing of setlists of Springsteen's concerts from 1999 onward is available at http://www.backstreets.com/setlists.html. A good selection of earlier setlists can be found in Charles R. Cross, ed., "Prove It All Night: Springsteen Performances 1965–89," in *Backstreets: Springsteen: The Man and His Music* (New York: Harmony Books, 1989), 167–218.

6. Springsteen, *Songs,* 26.

Chapter 3: A Romantic Rhapsody

1. Jon Landau, "Growing Young with Rock and Roll," *The Real Paper,* May 22, 1974, http://www.brucespringsteen.hu/docs/1974Landau.doc.

2. Marc Eliot, *Down Thunder Road: The Making of Bruce Springsteen* (New York: Simon & Schuster, 1992), 89–90.

3. Cross, ed., "Prove It All Night" in *Backstreets: Springsteen,* 173–74.

4. Eliot, *Down Thunder Road,* 118.

5. Ibid., 97.

6. Springsteen, *Songs,* 44.

7. Bruce Springsteen, *Wings for Wheels: The Making of "Born to Run,"* DVD (New York: Columbia Records, 2005).

8. Marsh, *Born to Run,* 132.

9. *Wings for Wheels: The Making of "Born to Run,"* a DVD included as part of the boxed set released by Columbia Records to celebrate the thirtieth anniversary of the release of *Born to Run,* provides a fascinating, behind-the-scenes look at the arduous process of completing Springsteen's third album.

10. Marsh, *Born to Run,* 135.

11. Jessica Kaye and Richard Brewer, eds., *Meeting across the River: Stories Inspired by the Haunting Bruce Springsteen Song* (New York: Bloomsbury USA, 2005).

Chapter 4: Maintaining Integrity

1. Marsh, *Born to Run*, 158.
2. Greil Marcus, review of *Born to Run, Rolling Stone,* October 9, 1975, http://www.rollingstone.com/reviews/album/171750/review/6068058/borntorun.
3. Marsh, *Born to Run*, 168.
4. Christopher Sandford, *Springsteen Point Blank* (Cambridge, MA: Da Capo Press, 1999), 127.
5. Springsteen, *Songs*, 66.
6. Ibid., 69.
7. Ibid., 65.
8. Sandford, *Springsteen Point Blank*, 122.
9. Chadbourne A. Spring, "It Can Be Said That Only Man Grieves," in ed. Carl Seaburg, *Great Occasions: Readings for the Celebration of Birth, Coming-of-Age, Marriage, and Death* (Boston: Skinner House Books, 1988), 189–90.
10. Dorothy Soelle, *To Work and to Love: A Theology of Creation* (Philadelphia: Fortress Press, 1984), 139.
11. See James Hillman, *The Soul's Code: In Search of Character and Calling* (New York: Random House, 1996).

Chapter 5: Life Keeps On Rollin' Along

1. Recording Industry of America, "Gold and Platinum: Top 100 Albums," http://www.riaa.com/gp/bestsellers/topalbums.asp.
2. Marsh, *Born to Run*, 206.
3. Ibid.
4. Ibid., 209.
5. Ibid.
6. Geoffrey Cowley, "Is Love the Best Drug?" *Newsweek*, March 16, 1998.
7. Springsteen, *Songs*, 101.
8. James Baldwin in "Selected Quotes about Change," *Quotatio: 50,000+ Quotations,* http://www.quotatio.com/topics/change.html.

Chapter 6: Facing Sin and Evil

1. Dave Marsh, *Glory Days: Bruce Springsteen in the 1980s* (New York: Pantheon Books, 1987), 103.
2. Sandford, *Point Blank*, 193.
3. Ibid., 194.
4. Marsh, *Glory Days*, 105.
5. Ibid., 102.
6. As noted, Starkweather actually murdered *eleven* people in Nebraska and Wyoming between December 1957 and February 1958.
7. Thich Nhat Hahn, *Peace Is Every Step: The Path of Mindfulness in Everyday Life.* New York: Bantam, 1991. Also available at http://www.abuddhistlibrary .com/Buddhism/G%20-%20TNH/TNH/From%20An%20Evening%20with%20

Thich%20Nhat%20Hahn/From%20An%20Evening%20with%20Thich%20Nh
at%20Hahn.rtf.

Chapter 7: American Ambiguity

1. Marsh, *Glory Days*, 152.
2. Ibid., 159.
3. Ibid., 105.
4. Ibid., 73.
5. Ibid., 75.
6. Geoffrey Himes, *Born in the U.S.A.* (New York: Continuum, 2005), 9.
7. Marsh, *Glory Days*, 116.
8. Ibid.
9. George Will, "Yankee Doodle Springsteen," *Washington Post*, September 13, 1984, reprinted in *Racing in the Street: The Bruce Springsteen Reader*, ed. June Skinner Sawyers (New York: Penguin Books, 2004), 108–9.
10. Todd Leopold, "Analysis: The Age of Reagan," *CNN.com*, June 16, 2004, http://www.cnn.com/2004/SHOWBIZ/06/16/reagan.80s/index.html.
11. Himes, *Born in the U.S.A.*, 111.
12. Springsteen, *Songs*, 165.
13. Ibid., 166.

Chapter 8: Overcoming the Long Loneliness

1. Nielson Business Media, Inc. "Historical Charts." http://www.billboard
.com/bbcom/charts/yearend_chart_index.jsp.
2. Hank Bordowitz, *The Bruce Springsteen Scrapbook* (New York: Citadel Press, 2004), 97.
3. It would not be surpassed in this regard until Garth Brooks released his *Double Live* set in 1999.
4. Sandford, *Point Blank*, 270.
5. Scialfa had officially joined the E Street Band just before the *Born in the U.S.A.* tour in 1984.
6. Springsteen, *Songs*, 216.
7. Ibid., 217.
8. Often considered together because of their simultaneous release, the albums are sometimes referred to by Springsteen fans by the common name, not necessarily complimentary, *Lucky Touch*. *Human Touch* debuted on the *Billboard* charts at number three, and the more critically acclaimed *Lucky Town* at number two, but both quickly faded from view after that.
9. The two songs that do not fit this criteria are "The Big Muddy" and "Souls of the Departed." "Local Hero" may be a stretch, although it is certainly autobiographical.
10. Marsh, *Born to Run*, 14.

Chapter 9: Seeking Justice

1. The lineup included Patti Scialfa and—for the first time—*both* Steven Van Zandt and Nils Lofgren, as well as Springsteen himself, of course, on guitars.

2. *Greatest Hits* was released on February 27, 1995. The video *Blood Brothers* (New York: Columbia Music Video, 1996) provides a fascinating account of these recording sessions.

3. Anders Osterling, "Presentation Speech, The Nobel Prize In Literature, 1962: John Steinbeck," http://nobelprize.org/nobel_prizes/literature/laureates/1962/press.html.

4. Springsteen contributed a live recording to the album of his cover of the song "Trapped" by Jimmy Cliff.

5. It also received four Grammy awards, including one for "Song of the Year"—the only song by Springsteen ever to be so honored.

6. Springsteen, *Songs*, 274.

7. Ibid., 276.

Chapter 10: From Good Friday to Easter

1. Christopher Phillips, "*Tracks* Brings Bruce to Europe," *Backstreets*, Winter 1998, 9.

2. Richard Tafoya, "Springsteen Ticket Sales Prompt Record-Setting Arena Stay," *liveDaily*, May 24, 1999, http://www.livedaily.com/news/Springsteen_Ticket_Sales_Prompt_RecordSetting_Arena_Stay-322.html. A total of 308,000 tickets were sold for the shows at the East Rutherford, N.J., venue. An average of 15,000 tickets were sold per minute, establishing an industry record for consecutive large-venue performances.

3. Chris Willman, review of *Bruce Springsteen and the E Street Band: Live in New York City, EW.com*, April 9, 2001, http://www.ew.com/ew/article/0,,105584,00.html.

4. Sandy Carter, "Bruce Springsteen's Land of Hope and Dreams," *Z Magazine*, December 1999, http://www.zmag.org/zmag//articles/dec1999carter.htm.

5. Eric Alterman, "Rock and Roll Fantasies," *Nation,* July 17, 2000, http://www.thenation.com/doc/20000717/alterman.

6. Robert Hilburn, "Under the Boss' Skin," *Los Angeles Times*, April 1, 2001, http://frankenschulz.de/bruce/under-the-boss-skin.html.

7. Josh Tyrangiel and Kate Carcaterra, "Bruce Rising," *Time*, August 5, 2002, http://www.time.com/time/magazine/article/0,9171,1002987,00.html.

8. Dave Marsh, *Bruce Springsteen on Tour, 1968–2005* (New York: Bloomsbury USA, 2006), 254.

9. Tyrangiel and Carcaterra, "Bruce Rising."

10. Marsh, *Bruce Springsteen on Tour*, 237.

11. Thomas Wolfe, *You Can't Go Home Again* (New York: Harper & Brothers, 1940), quoted in "Some Things Will Never Change," *Singing the Living Tradition* (Boston: Beacon Press, 1993), 561–62.

12. Andrew E. Massimino and Christopher Phillips, "Behind the Songs," *Backstreets*, Fall 2002, 19.

13. Dave Marsh posits that the song concerns a Muslim woman and an American soldier; see Marsh, *Bruce Springsteen on Tour*, 262.

14. Massimino and Phillips, "Behind the Songs," 25.

15. Quoted in ibid., 23.

16. "The cross of my calling" which the protagonist in this song wears is a fireman's cross, not that of a member of the Christian clergy. For a thorough explication of the firefighters' imagery in "The Rising" see Philip Hausler, "Wheels of Fire," *Backstreets*, Fall 2002, 24.

Chapter 11: Citizen Springsteen

1. Cited in Ray Waddell, "As Tour Ends, Boss Remains King of the Road," Reuters, October 11, 2003, http://www.springsteen.net/nyheter.php?id=160.

2. Christopher Phillips, "Top Prizes Elude *The Rising*," *Backstreets,* Winter 2002–Spring 2003, 8.

3. In actuality, the night was hardly all bad for Bruce: Springsteen won three of the five awards for which he was nominated: Best Rock Album, Best Rock Song, and Best Male Rock Vocal.

4. Others besides Springsteen and the E Street Band participating in the Vote for Change tour included Bright Eyes, Jackson Browne, Tracy Chapman, Crosby, Stills, and Nash, the Dave Matthews Band, Death Cab for Cutie, the Dixie Chicks, Kenny "Babyface" Edmonds, John Fogerty, Peter Frampton, Ben Harper, Jack Johnson, Jurassic 5, Keb Mo, My Morning Jacket, Pearl Jam, Bonnie Raitt, R.E.M., Gob Roberts, James Taylor, and Neil Young.

5. "Vote for Change: Artists' Declaration," *MoveonPac.org*, http://pol.moveon.org/vfc/artistsdeclaration.html.

6. Marsh, *Bruce Springsteen on Tour*, 269.

7. Ibid., 272.

8. Bruce Springsteen, "Chords for Change," *New York Times*, August 5, 2004, http://www.nytimes.com/2004/08/05/opinion/05bruce.html?ex=1249444800 &en=7686675ef1018abe&ei=5090.

9. Springsteen, *VH1 Storytellers: Bruce Springsteen*.

10. Bruce Springsteen, interview by Renee Montagne, *Morning Edition*, NPR, April 26, 2005.

11. Matthew Orel, "From Adam to Jesus: Springsteen's Use of Scripture," unpublished paper presented at Glory Days: A Bruce Springsteen Symposium, sponsored by Penn State University, held at Monmouth University, West Long Branch, NJ, September 9–11, 2005.

12. Christopher Phillips, "The Devil's in the Details," *Backstreets*, Winter 2005/2006, 51.

13. Jon Parales, "Bruce Almighty," *New York Times*, April 24, 2005, http://www.nytimes.com/2005/04/24/arts/music/24pare.html.

14. Indeed, the writing of all of the songs on *Devils & Dust* preceded the 2004 election by more than a year.

15. For instance, the song "My Beautiful Reward," also from the period around 1991, has its protagonist "crashing down like a drunk on a barroom floor."

16. Parales, "Bruce Almighty," *New York Times*, April 24, 2005, http://www.nytimes.com/2005/04/24/arts/music/24pare.html.

17. The song "Black Cowboys" was largely inspired by Jonathan Kozol's study of the children of Mott Haven: *Amazing Grace: The Lives of Children and the Conscience of a Nation* (New York: Crown, 1995).

18. Phillips, "Devil's in the Details," 60.

19. Jon Bream, "Springsteen: The Man and His Fans," *Minneapolis Star Tribune*, May 10, 2005, 1E.

20. Quoted by Phillips, "Devil's in the Details," 56.

Chapter 12: Coming Home Again

1. George Orwell, "Politics and the English Language," *George Orwell (1903–1950),* http://www.orwell.ru/library/essays/politics/english/e_polit.

2. John Kerry, "Vietnam Veterans against the War Statement by John Kerry to the Senate Committee of Foreign Relations, April 23, 1971," *The Sixties Project,* http://www3.iath.virginia.edu/sixties/HTML_docs/Resources/Primary/Manifestos/VVAW_Kerry_Senate.html.

3. "Iraq Coalition Casualty Count," http://icasualties.org/oif.

4. Bruce Springsteen, "The Rolling Stone Interview: Bruce Springsteen," by Joe Levy, *Rolling Stone,* November 1, 2007, 52.

5. A. O. Scott, "In Love with Pop, Uneasy with the World," *New York Times Online Edition,* September 30, 2007, http://www.nytimes.com/2007/09/30/arts/music/30scot.html.

6. Harry Browne, "Sinister Magic," *Counterpunch,* http://www.counterpunch.org, September 25, 2007, http://www.counterpunch.org/browne09252007.html.

7. Scott Pelley, interview with Bruce Springsteen, *60 Minutes,* CBS, October 7, 2007.

8. Stan Friedman, "Glimpses of God, " *Christianity Today Online,* http://www.christianitytoday.com/music/glimpses/2007/magic.html.

Conclusion: Bruce's Ten Suggestions for Spiritual Living

1. Andrew M. Greeley, "The Catholic Imagination of Bruce Springsteen," *America,* February 6, 1998, reprinted in June Skinner Sawyers, ed., *Racing in the Street: The Bruce Springsteen Reader* (New York: Penguin Books, 2004). 159–60.

2. "This Hard Land" was cut from the final lineup of *Born in the U.S.A.,* largely at the insistence of Jon Landau, who wanted Springsteen to include another "hit single." The song was later released on Springsteen's *Greatest Hits*

album, and an earlier version from the *Born in the U.S.A.* sessions was also included on Springsteen's multivolume *Tracks* set in 1998. Drummer Max Weinberg called "This Hard Land" his favorite song the band had ever cut. See Cross, *Backstreets: Springsteen,* 162).

    3. Parales, "Bruce Almighty."

Bibliography

Alterman, Eric. *It Ain't No Sin to Be Glad You're Alive: The Promise of Bruce Springsteen.* Boston: Little, Brown, 1999.
————. "Rock and Roll Fantasies." *Nation,* July 17, 2000, http://www.thenation.com/oc/20000717/alterman.
Bangs, Lester. Review of *Greetings from Asbury Park, N.J.* by Bruce Springsteen. *Rolling Stone,* July 5, 1973, http://www.rollingstone.com/reviews/album/107193/review/5943460/greetingsfromasburyparknj.
Bordowitz, Hank. *The Bruce Springsteen Scrapbook.* New York: Citadel Press, 2004.
Bream, Jon. "Springsteen: The Man and His Fans." *Minneapolis Star Tribune,* May 10, 2005, 1E.
Browne, Harry. "Sinister Magic." *Counterpunch,* September 25, 2007. http://www. counterpunch.org/browne09252007.html.
Carter, Sandy. "Bruce Springsteen's Land of Hope and Dreams." *Z Magazine,* December 1999. http://www.zmag.org/zmag//articles/dec1999carter.htm.
Cavicchi, Daniel. *Tramps Like Us: Music and Meaning among Springsteen Fans.* New York: Oxford University Press, 1998.
Cocks, Jay. "Rock's New Sensation: The Backstreet Phantom of Rock." *Time,* October 27, 1975, http://www.time.com/time/magazine/article/0,9171,913583,00.html.
Coles, Robert. *Bruce Springsteen's America: The People Listening, a Poet Singing.* New York: Random House, 2003.
Cross, Charles R., ed. *Backstreets: Springsteen, the Man and His Music.* New York: Harmony Books, 1989.
Eliot, Marc. *Down Thunder Road: The Making of Bruce Springsteen.* New York: Simon & Schuster, 1992.
Fricke, David. Review of *Magic* by Bruce Springsteen. *Rolling Stone,* October 18, 2007, http://www.rollingstone.com/reviews/album/16587992/review/16682049/magic.
Friedman, Stan. Review of *Magic* by Bruce Springsteen. *Christian Music Today,* http://www.christianitytoday.com/music/glimpses/2007/magic.html.

Graff, Gary. *The Ties That Bind: Bruce Springsteen A to E to Z.* Detroit: Visible Ink Press, 2005.

Graham, Renee. "The Boss Rules (The Man, That Is)." *Boston Globe*, August 13, 2002, 1E.

Greeley, Andrew M. "The Catholic Imagination of Bruce Springsteen." *America*, February 6, 1998, reprinted in *Racing in the Street: The Bruce Springsteen Reader*, ed. June Skinner Sawyers (New York: Penguin Books, 2004), 159–60.

Hausler, Philip. "Wheels of Fire." *Backstreets*, Fall 2002, 24.

Himes, Geoffrey. *Born in the U.S.A.* New York: Continuum, 2005.

Landau, Jon. "Growing Young with Rock and Roll." *Real Paper*, May 22, 1974, http://www.brucespringsteen.hu/docs/1974Landau.doc.

Leopold, Todd. "Analysis: The Age of Reagan." *CNN.com*, June 16, 2004, http://www.cnn.com/2004/SHOWBIZ/06/16/reagan.80s/index.html.

Lynch, Rich, Laura Lynch, and Pat Cacioppo. "Bruce Springsteen Rehearsals: These Shows Are Paramount Performances." *Kweevak.com Music Magazine*, April 28, 2005. http://www.kweevak.com/rd_art_2005_04_28_springsteen.php.

Marcus, Griel. Review of *Born to Run* by Bruce Springsteen. *Rolling Stone*, October 9, 1975, http://www.rollingstone.com/artists/brucespringsteen/albums/album/171750/review/6068058/born_to_run.

Marsh, Dave. *Born to Run: The Bruce Springsteen Story*, vol. 1. New York: Thunder's Mouth Press, 1996.

———. *Bruce Springsteen on Tour, 1968–2005.* New York: Bloomsbury USA, 2006.

———. *Glory Days: Bruce Springsteen in the 1980s.* New York: Pantheon Books, 1987.

Massimino, Andrew E., and Christopher Phillips. "Behind the Songs." *Backstreets*, Fall 2002, 19–25.

Morse, Steve. "The Quiet American." *Boston Globe*, May 19, 2005, http://www.boston.com/news/globe/living/articles/2005/05/19/the_quiet_american/.

Norris, Fred. "Bruce Springsteen Delivers on 'Promise.'" *VH1.com*, March 22, 1999.   http://www.vh1.com/artists/news/512970/19990322/springsteen_bruce.jhtml.

Orel, Matthew. "From Adam to Jesus: Springsteen's Use of Scripture." Unpublished paper presented at Glory Days: A Bruce Springsteen Symposium, sponsored by Penn State University, held at Monmouth University, West Long Branch, NJ, September 9–11, 2005.

Orth, Maureen, Janet Huck, and Peter S. Greenberg. "Making of a Rock Star." *Newsweek*, October 27, 1975, http://www.angelfire.com/rock3/jabongo/articles/Newsweek102775.html.

Parales, Jon. "Bruce Almighty." *New York Times*, April 24, 2005, http://www.nytimes.com/2005/04/24/arts/music/24pare.html.

Phillips, Christopher. "The Devil's in the Details." *Backstreets*, Winter 2005/2006, 51–60.

————. "Top Prizes Elude *The Rising*." *Backstreets,* Winter 2002–Spring 2003, 8–9.

————. "*Tracks* Brings Bruce to Europe." *Backstreets*, Winter 1998, 8–9.

Rose, Caryn. "Somerville Nights." *Backstreets*. Winter 2002–Spring 2003, 16–21.

Sandford, Christopher. *Springsteen Point Blank.* Cambridge, MA: Da Capo Press, 1999.

Santelli, Robert. *Greetings from E Street: The Story of Bruce Springsteen and the E Street Band.* San Francisco: Chronicle Books, 2006.

Sawyers, June Skinner, ed. *Racing in the Street: The Bruce Springsteen Reader.* New York: Penguin Books, 2004.

————. *Tougher than the Rest: 100 Best Bruce Springsteen Songs.* New York: Omnibus Press, 2006.

Scott, A. O. "In Love with Pop, Uneasy with the World." *New York Times Online Edition,* September 30, 2007, http://www.nytimes.com/2007/09/30/arts/music/30scot.html.

Springsteen, Bruce. "Chords for Change." *New York Times*, August 5, 2004, http://www.nytimes.com/2004/08/05/opinion/05bruce.html?ex=1249444800 &en=768bb75ef1018abe&ei=5090.

————. Interview by Renee Montagne. *Morning Edition*, NPR, April 26, 2005.

————. Interview by Scott Pelley. *60 Minutes,* CBS, October 7, 2007.

————. *Songs.* New York: Avon Books, 1998.

————. "The Rolling Stone Interview: Bruce Springsteen." By Kurt Loder. *Rolling Stone*, December 6, 1984, reprinted in Editors of Rolling Stone, *Bruce Springsteen: The Rolling Stone Files* (New York: Hyperion, 1996), 151–65.

————. "The Rolling Stone Interview: Bruce Springsteen." By Joe Levy. *Rolling Stone,* November 1, 2007, 50–56

————. *VH1 Storytellers: Bruce Springsteen.* DVD. New York: Columbia Music Video, 2005.

————. *Wings for Wheels: The Making of "Born to Run."* DVD. New York: Columbia Records, 2005.

Stratton, Christopher. "Springsteen and the Minor Prophets." *Notes on Music: Commentaries and Reviews.* http://www.explorefaith.com/music/spring steen.html.

Tafoya, Richard. "Springsteen Ticket Sales Prompt Record-Setting Arena Stay." *Live Daily*, May 24, 1999. http://www.livedaily.com/news/Springsteen_Ticket_Sales_Prompt_RecordSetting_Arena_Stay-322.html.

Tyrangiel, Josh, and Kate Carcaterra. "Bruce Rising." *Time*, August 5, 2002, http://www.time.com/time/magazine/article/0,9171,1002987,00.html.

"Vote for Change: Artists' Declaration." *MoveonPac.org*. http://pol.moveon.org/vfc/artistsdeclaration.html.

Ray Waddell. "As Tour Ends, Boss Remains King of the Road." Reuters, October 11, 2003. http://www.springsteen.net/nyheter.php?id=160.

Will, George. "Yankee Doodle Springsteen." *Washington Post*, September 13, 1984, reprinted in *Racing in the Street: The Bruce Springsteen Reader*, ed. June Skinner Sawyers (New York: Penguin Books, 2004), 107–9.

Willman, Chris. Review of *Bruce Springsteen and the E Street Band: Live in New York City*. *EW.com*. April 9, 2001. http://www.ew.com/ew/articl/0,,105584,00.html.

Wolff, Daniel. *Fourth of July, Asbury Park: A History of the Promised Land*. New York: Bloomsbury, 2005.